CISM Exam Prep

500+ Practice Questions

1st Edition

www.versatileread.com

Document Control

Proposal Name	:	CISM Exam Prep: +500 Practice Questions
Document Edition	:	1st
Document Release Date	:	21st May 2024
Reference	:	CISM
VR Product Code	:	20241402CISM

Feedback:
If you have any comments regarding the quality of this book or otherwise alter it to better suit your needs, you can contact us through email at info@versatileread.com

Please make sure to include the book's title and ISBN in your message.

About the Contributors:

Nouman Ahmed Khan

AWS/Azure/GCP-Architect, CCDE, CCIEx5 (R&S, SP, Security, DC, Wireless), CISSP, CISA, CISM, CRISC, ISO27K-LA is a Solution Architect working with a global telecommunication provider. He works with enterprises, mega-projects, and service providers to help them select the best-fit technology solutions. He also works as a consultant to understand customer business processes and helps select an appropriate technology strategy to support business goals. He has more than eighteen years of experience working with global clients. One of his notable experiences was his tenure with a large managed security services provider, where he was responsible for managing the complete MSSP product portfolio. With his extensive knowledge and expertise in various areas of technology, including cloud computing, network infrastructure, security, and risk management, Nouman has become a trusted advisor for his clients.

Abubakar Saeed

Abubakar Saeed is a trailblazer in the realm of technology and innovation. With a rich professional journey spanning over twenty-nine years, Abubakar has seamlessly blended his expertise in engineering with his passion for transformative leadership. Starting humbly at the grassroots level, he has significantly contributed to pioneering the Internet in Pakistan and beyond. Abubakar's multifaceted experience encompasses managing, consulting, designing, and implementing projects, showcasing his versatility as a leader.

His exceptional skills shine in leading businesses, where he champions innovation and transformation. Abubakar stands as a testament to the power of visionary leadership, heading operations, solutions design, and integration. His emphasis on adhering to project timelines and exceeding customer expectations has set him apart as a great leader. With an unwavering commitment to adopting technology for operational simplicity and enhanced efficiency, Abubakar Saeed continues to inspire and drive change in the industry.

Dr. Fahad Abdali

Dr. Fahad Abdali is an esteemed leader with an outstanding twenty-year track record in managing diverse businesses. With a stellar educational background, including a bachelor's degree from the prestigious NED University of Engineers & Technology and a Ph.D. from the University of Karachi, Dr. Abdali epitomizes academic excellence and continuous professional growth.

Dr. Abdali's leadership journey is marked by his unwavering commitment to innovation and his astute understanding of industry dynamics. His ability to navigate intricate challenges has driven growth and nurtured organizational triumph. Driven by a passion for excellence, he stands as a beacon of inspiration within the business realm. With his remarkable leadership skills, Dr. Fahad Abdali continues to steer businesses toward unprecedented success, making him a true embodiment of a great leader.

Muniza Kamran

Muniza Kamran is a technical content developer in a professional field. She crafts clear and informative content that simplifies complex technical concepts for diverse audiences, with a passion for technology. Her expertise lies in Microsoft, cybersecurity, cloud security and emerging technologies, making her a valuable asset in the tech industry. Her dedication to quality and accuracy ensures that her writing empowers readers with valuable insights and knowledge. She has done certification in SQL database, database design, cloud solution architecture, and NDG Linux unhatched from CISCO.

Table of Contents

About CISM Certification

Introduction

This section provides an introduction to the CISM (Certified Information Security Manager) certification, underscoring its pivotal role in the realm of IT governance, risk management, and security. It underscores the advantages of acquiring CISM certification, delineates the certification journey, and underscores the significance of upholding ethical standards. Furthermore, it delves into the growing demand for CISM-certified experts amidst the dynamic cybersecurity environment, laying the groundwork for subsequent discourse on exam readiness and professional pathways.

What is a CISM?

CISM stands for Certified Information Security Manager. ISACA (Information Systems Audit and Control Association) offers a certification that focuses on information security management. The CISM certification is designed for professionals who manage, design, oversee, and assess an enterprise's information security. It covers various aspects of information security governance, risk management, compliance, and incident management. Holding a CISM certification demonstrates a professional's commitment and expertise in information security management.

Benefits of CISM

Obtaining a CISM (Certified Information Security Manager) certification offers numerous benefits to professionals in the field of cybersecurity. Firstly, it significantly enhances career opportunities by opening doors to managerial and leadership roles within organizations. This certification validates expertise, showcasing proficiency in critical areas like governance, risk management, compliance, and incident response. Furthermore, CISM is globally recognized, providing credibility and increasing earning potential for certified individuals. Being part of a professional network of fellow CISM holders offers valuable collaboration, support, and knowledge sharing opportunities. Moreover, CISM-certified professionals are better equipped

to address the evolving challenges of information security within organizations, ensuring effective strategies, risk management, and compliance. Finally, maintaining CISM certification involves ongoing professional development, fostering continuous learning and staying updated with the latest trends and best practices in the field.

The CISM Certification Process

The CISM (Certified Information Security Manager) certification process involves several steps:

1. ***Meet Eligibility Requirements***: To be eligible for the CISM certification exam, candidates must have a minimum of five years of work experience in information security management, with at least three years of experience in three or more of the job practice analysis areas as defined by ISACA. Alternatively, candidates can substitute certain work experience with other qualifications or education.
2. ***Register for the Exam:*** Once eligibility requirements are met, candidates can register for the CISM exam through the ISACA website. It's essential to review the exam registration deadlines and requirements carefully.
3. ***Prepare for the Exam***: ISACA offers various resources to help candidates prepare for the CISM exam, including review courses, study materials, practice questions, and official publications. Many candidates also opt for self-study using textbooks and online resources.
4. ***Pass the Exam***: The CISM exam consists of 150 multiple-choice questions covering four domains: Information Security Governance, Information Risk Management, Information Security Program Development and Management, and Information Security Incident Management. Candidates must achieve a passing score to earn the certification.
5. ***Complete the Application for Certification***: After passing the exam, candidates must apply for certification. This includes providing work experience details and agreeing to adhere to the ISACA Code of Professional Ethics and Continuing Professional Education (CPE) Policy.

6. ***Adherence to the Code of Ethics:*** CISM holders must abide by the ISACA Code of Professional Ethics, which outlines standards of professional conduct and responsibilities in the field of information security management.
7. ***Continuing Professional Education (CPE)***: To maintain the CISM certification, holders must earn and report a minimum of 120 CPE hours over three years, with at least 20 CPE hours earned annually. This ensures that certified professionals stay current with advancements in the field and continue to enhance their knowledge and skills.

Experience Requirements

The experience required for the CISM (Certified Information Security Manager) certification consists of a minimum of five years of work experience in information security management. This experience should encompass a broad range of responsibilities and activities related to managing and overseeing an organization's information security program. Additionally, candidates must have acquired this experience within the ten years preceding the date of application for certification or within five years of passing the exam. ISACA, the organization that administers the CISM certification, defines specific job practice areas within information security management where candidates should have gained experience, such as governance, risk management, program development and management, and incident management. As outlined by ISACA's eligibility criteria, candidates can also substitute part of the required experience with relevant educational qualifications or security-related certifications. Meeting these experience requirements ensures that candidates have the necessary expertise and background to excel in information security management roles and successfully pursue the CISM certification.

ISACA Codes of Professional Ethics

The ISACA Code of Professional Ethics provides a guiding framework for CISM (Certified Information Security Manager) holders, emphasizing principles such as integrity, objectivity, confidentiality, and professional competence. CISM professionals are expected to uphold these ethical

standards in all facets of their work, including interactions with clients, employers, colleagues, and the broader community. This entails maintaining honesty and moral principles, avoiding conflicts of interest, safeguarding sensitive information, continuously enhancing professional knowledge and skills, and exercising due diligence in professional responsibilities. By adhering to the ISACA Code of Professional Ethics, CISM holders contribute to upholding the reputation and integrity of the information security profession while ensuring the effective management of information security risks. Violations of ethical principles may result in disciplinary actions, underlining the importance of ethical conduct in maintaining the trust and confidence of stakeholders.

The Certification Exam

The CISM (Certified Information Security Manager) certification exam is a comprehensive assessment of a candidate's knowledge and proficiency in information security management. The exam is designed to evaluate a candidate's understanding of key concepts, principles, and practices related to information security governance, risk management, program development and management, and incident management.

The CISM exam consists of 150 multiple-choice questions, which are distributed across the following four domains:

- **Information Security Governance:** This domain assesses a candidate's understanding of the establishment, implementation, and oversight of information security governance frameworks and processes within an organization.
- **Information Risk Management:** This domain evaluates a candidate's knowledge of risk management principles and practices, including risk assessment, analysis, mitigation, and monitoring.
- **Information Security Program Development and Management:** This domain focuses on the development, implementation, and management of information security programs, policies, procedures, and controls to protect organizational assets and meet business objectives.

- **Information Security Incident Management:** This domain assesses a candidate's ability to develop and implement incident response plans, identify and respond to security incidents, and effectively manage incident recovery and post-incident activities.

Candidates must demonstrate a deep understanding of these domains and their associated topics to pass the CISM exam. Achieving a passing score on the exam is a critical step towards earning the CISM certification and demonstrating proficiency in information security management.

Exam Preparation

Before Exam

Study the exam content, review study materials, take practice exams, create a study schedule, and join study groups. Familiarize yourself with the exam content outline provided by ISACA, which details the domains and topics covered in the exam. Utilize study materials such as textbooks, official ISACA publications, online courses, and practice exams to review key concepts and reinforce your understanding. Practice answering sample questions to assess your knowledge and identify areas that require further study. Develop a study schedule that allocates time for reviewing each domain and topic covered in the exam content outline. Consider joining study groups or forums where you can engage with other exam candidates, share resources, and discuss challenging topics.

Day of Exam

Arrive early, bring the required documents, stay calm and focused, and manage your time. Arrive at the exam center well before the scheduled start time to allow for check-in procedures. Bring valid identification documents and any other required materials specified by the exam center. Try to remain calm and focused during the exam. Take deep breaths and read each question carefully before selecting your answer. Pace yourself throughout the exam to ensure you have enough time to answer all questions. Flag difficult questions for review if necessary.

After Exam

Reflect on your performance, review missed questions, continue learning, and await results. Take some time to reflect on your performance in the exam. Identify areas where you felt confident and areas where you may need to improve. If you have access to your exam results, review any questions you missed to understand why you answered incorrectly and learn from your mistakes. Regardless of the exam outcome, continue to stay updated with developments in the field of information security management. Attend training sessions, workshops, and conferences to expand your knowledge and skills. Await the official results from ISACA, which typically arrive within a few weeks of taking the exam. Use this time to relax and recharge after the intense preparation and exam experience.

Exam Information

Certified Information Security Manager

Prior Certification **No**	Exam Validity **3 Years**
Exam Fee **$575 for ISACA members** **$760 for non-members**	Exam Duration **240 Minutes**
No. of Questions **150**	Passing Marks **450/800 points**

Recommended Experience
Five years of infosec management experience, managerial skills, ISACA framework knowledge, and ideally, a related education.

Exam Format
Multiple Choice Questions.

Languages
English, Chinese, Japanese, and Spanish.

Retaining your Certified Information Security Manager (CISM)

Maintaining your CISM (Certified Information Security Manager) certification involves fulfilling certain requirements set forth by ISACA (Information Systems Audit and Control Association) to ensure that certified professionals remain up-to-date with developments in the field of information security management. Here's how you can retain your CISM certification:

Continuing Education

Continuing Professional Education (CPE) refers to the ongoing learning and professional development activities that individuals pursue to maintain and enhance their knowledge, skills, and expertise in a particular field. In the context of certifications such as CISM (Certified Information Security Manager), CPE refers to activities that certified professionals undertake to stay current with developments, best practices, and emerging trends in information security management. Examples of CPE activities include attending conferences, workshops, seminars, webinars, training courses, completing self-study programs, participating in industry-related projects, and engaging in knowledge-sharing activities such as mentoring or teaching.

CPE Maintenance Fees

CPE Maintenance Fees are fees paid by certified professionals to maintain their certification status. These fees are typically paid annually to the certifying organization, such as ISACA, for the CISM certification. The maintenance fees contribute to the administration and maintenance of the certification program, including processing CPE submissions, providing resources and support to certified professionals, upholding certification standards, and ensuring the ongoing relevance and credibility of the certification. Failure to pay the required maintenance fees may result in the loss of certification status.

Revocation of Certificate

The revocation of a certificate, such as the CISM (Certified Information Security Manager) certification, signifies the withdrawal of an individual's certification status by the certifying organization. This action is taken in response to serious violations of the certification program's policies, code of ethics, or standards of professional conduct. Reasons for revocation may include engaging in unethical behavior, criminal conduct, misuse of the certification, or non-compliance with program requirements. The revocation process typically involves investigating the allegations against the individual and determining if they warrant revocation. If the allegations are substantiated, the certifying organization may revoke the individual's

certification status, leading to the loss of the right to use the certification designation and potential professional consequences. While revocation is a serious matter, certifying organizations may have appeals processes in place for individuals who wish to contest the decision.

CISM Exam Preparation Pointers

Preparing for the CISM (Certified Information Security Manager) exam requires a structured approach to cover the breadth of topics and domains outlined by ISACA. Here are some pointers to guide your exam preparation effectively:

- **Understand the Exam Content**: Familiarize yourself with the CISM exam content outline provided by ISACA. This outline details the domains and topics covered in the exam, helping you understand what to expect and prioritize during your preparation.
- **Use Official Study Materials:** Utilize official study materials provided by ISACA, including textbooks, review manuals, and practice exams. These resources are specifically designed to align with the exam content and provide a comprehensive understanding of key concepts.
- **Create a Study Plan:** Develop a study plan that outlines the domains and topics you need to cover and allocates time for each area. Set realistic study goals and deadlines to ensure consistent progress leading up to the exam.
- **Practice with Sample Questions:** Practice answering sample questions to familiarize yourself with the exam format and assess your understanding of key concepts. ISACA offers official practice exams that closely simulate the actual exam experience.
- **Focus on Weak Areas:** Identify areas where you feel less confident or have limited experience and prioritize studying those topics. Allocate additional study time to strengthen your understanding and proficiency in these areas.
- **Join Study Groups or Forums:** Consider joining study groups or online forums where you can interact with other exam candidates, share resources, and discuss challenging topics. Engaging with peers can provide valuable insights and support during your preparation.

- **Review and Reinforce:** Regularly review the material you have studied and reinforce your understanding by explaining concepts to others or teaching them to yourself. Use different study techniques such as flashcards, mind maps, or mnemonic devices to enhance retention.
- **Simulate Exam Conditions:** Prior to the exam, simulate exam conditions by taking full-length practice exams under timed conditions. This helps you build endurance, manage time effectively, and familiarize yourself with the pressure of the exam environment.
- **Stay Calm and Confident:** Maintain a positive attitude and confidence in your preparation efforts. Trust in your knowledge and abilities, and remember to take breaks and manage stress to stay focused and refreshed during the exam.
- **Review Exam Policies and Procedures:** Familiarize yourself with exam policies and procedures, including registration deadlines, exam format, and rules for exam day. Ensure you have all the necessary documentation and understand what to expect on the day of the exam.

By following these pointers and maintaining a disciplined approach to your exam preparation, you can increase your chances of success in achieving the CISM certification.

Job Opportunities with CISM Certifications

Obtaining a Certified Information Security Manager (CISM) certification can open up various job opportunities in the field of information security and cybersecurity. Here are some roles where CISM certification is highly valued:

Information Security Manager

As the name suggests, this role involves overseeing an organization's security policies and procedures, managing security teams, and ensuring compliance with regulations. CISM certification is particularly relevant for this position because it demonstrates expertise in managing, designing, and assessing an enterprise's information security program.

Cybersecurity Consultant

Many consulting firms seek professionals with CISM certification to provide expert advice on cybersecurity strategy, risk management, and compliance. Consultants with CISM credentials can work with a range of clients across different industries to assess their security posture and recommend improvements.

Security Architect

Security architects design and implement security systems to protect an organization's IT infrastructure. They need to have a deep understanding of security principles and technologies, making CISM certification valuable for this role. Security architects often work closely with other IT teams to ensure that security measures are integrated seamlessly into the organization's systems and applications.

Security Analyst/Engineer

Security analysts and engineers are responsible for monitoring networks and systems for security breaches, investigating incidents, and implementing security solutions. CISM certification can enhance their credibility and demonstrate their ability to analyze security risks and develop appropriate mitigation strategies.

Risk Manager

Risk managers assess and mitigate risks to an organization's information assets. They work closely with business leaders to identify potential threats and vulnerabilities and develop strategies to manage them effectively. CISM certification provides risk managers with the necessary skills and knowledge to assess security risks and develop risk management plans.

Compliance Officer

Compliance officers ensure that an organization complies with relevant laws, regulations, and industry standards related to information security. CISM certification demonstrates expertise in developing and implementing security policies and procedures to meet compliance requirements.

Chief Information Security Officer (CISO)

CISOs are senior executives responsible for overseeing an organization's overall security strategy and ensuring that security initiatives align with business objectives. CISM certification is highly beneficial for aspiring CISOs as it demonstrates their ability to manage and lead a comprehensive information security program.

These are a few examples of the many job opportunities available to individuals with CISM certification. The demand for cybersecurity professionals continues to grow, and obtaining relevant certifications such as CISM can significantly enhance your career prospects in this field.

Demand for CISA Certification in 2024

The demand for CISM certification is also strong in 2024, and here is why:

- **High Priority for Businesses:** Cybersecurity remains a top concern for organizations as cyberattacks continue to rise. Businesses need skilled professionals to lead and manage their information security programs. The CISM certification demonstrates an individual's capability to acheive precisely that.
- **Top-Paying Credential:** CISM consistently ranks among the highest-paying IT certifications, with an average salary exceeding $156,000, according to recent reports. This high earning potential makes it a desirable credential for career advancement.
- **Specialized Expertise:** While certifications like CISSP focus on broad cybersecurity knowledge, CISM offers a specialized focus on information security management. This targeted expertise is valuable for businesses seeking security leaders.

Practice Questions

1. What is the role of the Information Security Steering Committee as per the governance roles and responsibilities?

A) Directs and coordinates implementation of information security program

B) Provides management, operational, and technical controls

C) Establishes and supports security program

D)Classifies and establishes requirements for safeguarding information assets

2. Which one of the following is NOT one of the three key elements necessary for successful security and privacy policies and procedures?

A) Documented

B) Communicated

C) Updated Annually

D) Current

3. What is meant by 'two-factor authentication'?

A) Using two different passwords

B) Using a password and another method, such as a token card or biometric

C) Requiring two people to authenticate an action

D) Changing the password twice for security

4. What does 'least privilege' mean in the context of authorization?

A) Minimum level of access privileges required for users

B) The least number of users with access to sensitive information

C) Basic user privileges that all employees must have

D) Restricting user privileges to the maximum extent

5. What is the primary purpose of a Business Continuity Plan (BCP)?

A) To recover lost data

B) To sustain essential business operations during a disruption

C) To respond to cyber incidents

D) To recover from a physical threat to property

6. What is the main difference between Business Continuity Planning (BCP) and Disaster Recovery Planning (DRP)?

A) BCP focuses on IT systems, while DRP focuses on business processes

B) BCP is for short-term disruptions, while DRP is for long-term recovery

C) BCP is a corporate requirement, while DRP is an IT function

D) BCP includes data backup, while DRP includes business process mapping

7. What is the recommended frequency for testing Business Continuity and Disaster Recovery plans?

A) Biennially

B) Semi-annually

C) Quarterly

D) Annually

8. Who is responsible for establishing the security posture and strategy for activities such as firewall administration and encryption?

A) Business Unit Managers

B) Chief Information Security Officer (CISO)

C) Information Security Staff

D) IT Department

9. Which of the following is NOT a type of control mentioned as part of an effective information security strategy?

A) Preventive

B) Detective

C) Containment

D) Enforcement

10. What is the purpose of a Service Level Agreement (SLA) in the context of an information security strategy?

A) To establish a communication plan

B) To define the information access levels

C) To identify service levels and recovery requirements

D) To document the security program goals

11. What is the primary reason that Business Continuity Planning (BCP) and Disaster Recovery Planning (DRP) fail?

A) Lack of technology

B) Inadequate funding

C) Lack of internal risk assessment

D) Poor communication with stakeholders

12. Which of the following is NOT a requirement for having a security program?

A) HIPAA

B) GLBA

C) Sarbanes-Oxley

D) FCC

13. What comprises the fiduciary duty of management in protecting the assets of an organization?

A) Duty of loyalty and duty of care

B) Duty of confidentiality and duty of honesty

C) Duty of transparency and duty of efficiency

D) Duty of profitability and duty of sustainability

14. What is due diligence in the context of information security governance?

A) The process of training employees on security practices

B) The process of systematically evaluating information to identify risks

C) The act of updating security software and hardware regularly

D) The enforcement of security policies and procedures

15. How can senior management demonstrate their commitment to information security?

A) By outsourcing IT security

B) By wearing their employee identification badges

C) By cutting the information security budget

D) By ignoring international standards

16. What should information security responsibilities be tied to in an organization?

A) Only the IT department's objectives

B) The company's marketing strategies

C) Each employee's job description and performance objectives

D) The organization's social media policies

17. By law and international standards, who is responsible for approving security policies and plans?

A) Individual employees

B) The Information Security Steering Committee (ISSC)

C) External auditors

D) Third-party consultants

18. What is the ultimate responsibility of senior management in the context of a security program?

A) Delegating tasks to IT departments

B) Protecting the assets of the organization

C) Implementing the latest technology

D) Reducing operational costs

19. What must senior management witness and have demonstrated in relation to information security goals and objectives?

A) Decreased operational expenses

B) Increased sales figures

C) How these goals and objectives will be met

D) A reduction in the IT department's headcount

20. What is the importance of incorporating information security into the employee standards of conduct document?

A) It helps in marketing the company's products

B) It provides a reference for financial auditing

C) It defines unacceptable activities and consequences for non-compliance

D) It serves as a guideline for customer service protocols

21. Who is ultimately responsible for meeting business objectives or mission requirements?

A) Chief Information Security Officer (CISO)

B) Senior Management

C) Business Managers

D) Information Security Officer

22. What is the role of the Chief Information Security Officer (CISO) in an organization?

A) To ensure compliance with security regulations

B) To be the functional owner of organization assets

C) To manage the organization's security programs

D) To handle the planning, budgeting, and performance of information security components

23. What is meant by the term "Information Owner"?

A) A person who installs security software

B) The individual responsible for the organization's security programs

C) Department managers who ensure controls are in place for their information resources

D) The person who physically owns the information assets

24. What is the responsibility of Business Managers in the context of information security governance?

A) To execute the organization's security programs

B) To make cost-benefit decisions to ensure protection of assets

C) To conduct annual performance reviews of employees

D) To develop risk assessment capabilities

25. How should employee compliance with security regulations be evaluated according to the text?

A) Through direct observation

B) As a factor in their annual performance appraisal

C) By the number of security incidents reported

D) Based on customer feedback

26. Why is it important for information security to work with human resources?

A) To manage risk assessment and risk management projects

B) To ensure security-related competencies are included in job descriptions

C) To conduct security training sessions

D) To monitor employee behavior

27. What should be established in the asset classification policy?

A) The risk assessment results

B) The term "owner" for department managers

C) The details of the organization's security programs

D) The annual performance appraisal criteria

28. Who is responsible for the organization's security programs and risk management?

A) Senior Management

B) Information Owner

C) Information Security Officer

D) Chief Information Security Officer (CISO)

29. What are the responsibilities associated with the role of 'owner' within the context of security governance?

A) To maintain the security software up-to-date

B) To conduct regular security audits

C) To fulfill the fiduciary responsibility of management to protect assets

D) To train employees on security best practices

30. How should resources be applied according to senior management's responsibilities?

A) Arbitrarily to any department that requests them

B) Solely based on the CISO's recommendations

C) Effectively to develop capabilities to meet mission requirements

D) Equally across all departments, regardless of need

31. What are the two key responsibilities assigned to management concerning information security?

A) Policy implementation and risk assessment

B) Access control and disaster recovery planning

C) Fiduciary duty and due diligence

D) Security auditing and compliance monitoring

32. Why is it not recommended for information security to report to the operations department?

A) Operations may not have the necessary security expertise

B) Operations may prioritize production schedules over security controls

C) Operations are solely responsible for disaster recovery planning

D) Operations typically handle only physical security

33. What did the National Cyber Security Summit Task Force publish in 2004?

A) National Agenda for Information Security in 2006

B) Cyber Security Industry Alliance

C) Information Security Governance: A Call to Action

D) Corporate Governance Task Force Report

34. What shift necessitated the reassessment of the location of information protection activity?

A) The transition from desktop-based computing to mobile devices

B) The shift from mainframe data centers to decentralized client/server environments

C) The change from paper-based to digital records

D) The movement from in-house IT to outsourced cloud services

35. Which department should information security ideally report to for autonomy and effectiveness?

A) Auditing

B) Operations

C) Physical Security

D) Chief Information Security Officer (CISO)

36. What is the primary responsibility of the computer security group mentioned in the text?

A) Setting security policy for the entire organization

B) Conducting independent annual audits

C) Access control and disaster recovery planning

D) Reviewing cyber security measures at board meetings

37. What did the Cyber Security Industrial Alliance recommend in 2005?

A) CEOs should ignore cyber security measures

B) The federal government should mandate cyber security reviews

C) CEOs should review cyber security measures at board meetings

D) Information security should report to physical security

38. Why is reporting information security to auditing considered a conflict of interest?

A) It would result in an overlap of security policy setting

B) Auditing requires separate access controls

C) It mixes the roles of making laws and judging compliance

D) Auditing is not involved in information security

39. What is a significant change in focus regarding the function of information security?

A) It is no longer a support function but a main business operation

B) It is solely the responsibility of the IT department

C) It is no longer considered an IT function but a business and governance issue

D) It has shifted from a governance issue to a technical challenge

40. According to the text, why is it crucial for senior management to support an information security program?

A) To ensure that the program is limited to IT-related risks

B) To comply with the Cyber Security Industry Alliance's mandates

C) To demonstrate compliance with fiduciary duty and due diligence requirements

D) To focus solely on the technical aspects of security

41. What is the primary goal of the Information Systems Security Association (ISSA)?

A) To serve as a centralized source of information and guidance in the field of auditing controls

B) To promote management practices ensuring the confidentiality, integrity, and availability of information resources

C) To provide a full schedule of training classes on encryption and intrusion management

D) To publish the annual CSI/FBI Computer Crime and Security Survey

42. What is the role of Information Security within an enterprise according to the enterprisewide policy documents?

A) To provide a full schedule of training classes on various security topics

B) To assess the adequacy of financial controls within the organization

C) To direct and support the protection of information assets from various threats

D) To serve and train the information, computer, and network security professionals

43. Which statement best describes the Information Systems Audit and Control Association (ISACA)?

A) It is solely dedicated to training the information, computer, and network security professional.

B) It is a not-for-profit, international organization of information security professionals and practitioners.

C) It is the world's leading membership organization for IT governance and control.

D) It is the largest international, not-for-profit association specifically for security professionals.

44. What does the annual report on the state of information security typically include?

A) A discussion on the enterprise's shared beliefs and due diligence concepts

B) A report on the levels of compliance seen throughout the business units

C) The results of a standard feature audit performed by the audit staff

D) An automated, standards-based security program assessment

45. According to the enterprisewide policy document, what is a crucial element for the enterprise in making business decisions?

A) Implementing a formal risk analysis process to document all management decisions

B) Establishing a variety of information protection policies and procedures

C) Enforcing employee compliance to information protection-related issues as an annual appraisal element

D) Maintaining active membership in the Computer Security Institute (CSI)

46. What is the approximate budget allocation for Information Protection (IP) within an overall Information Security Office (ISO) budget?

A) 1-3% of the overall ISO budget

B) 5-10% of the overall ISO budget

C) 10-15% of the overall ISO budget

D) 20-25% of the overall ISO budget

47. What is the recommended frequency for reviewing and modifying the Information Protection (IP) program?

A) Biannually

B) Quarterly

C) Monthly

D) Annually

48. Which organization was originally formed as the EDP Auditors Association?

A) Information Systems Security Association (ISSA)

B) Computer Security Institute (CSI)

C) Information Systems Audit and Control Association (ISACA)

D) International Information Systems Security Certification Consortium $(ISC)^2$

49. What is the purpose of the annual CSI/FBI Computer Crime and Security Survey?

A) To assess the administrative and operational effectiveness of organizational units

B) To provide a centralized source of information and guidance in the field of IT governance

C) To serve and train the information, computer, and network security professional

D) To aggressively advocate the critical importance of protecting information assets

50. Who is typically responsible for preparing the annual report on the state of information security?

A) The Chief Information Officer (CIO)

B) The Corporate Information Protection Coordinator

C) The Chief Information Security Officer (CISO)

D) The head of the audit staff

51. What is the primary purpose of the Gramm–Leach–Bliley Act (GLBA)?

A) To create a national data privacy law.

B) To provide privacy of customer information by financial service organizations.

C) To establish mandatory punishment for computer-related crimes.

D) To make trade secret theft a federal crime.

52. Which act requires companies to have due diligence programs with internal controls and enforcement to avoid liability?

A) The Economic Espionage Act of 1996

B) The Foreign Corrupt Practices Act (FCPA)

C) The Sarbanes–Oxley Act (SOX)

D) The Health Insurance Portability and Accountability Act (HIPAA)

53. What does the term 'fiduciary duty' refer to in corporate governance?

A) The obligation to enforce policies and procedures consistently.

B) The responsibility of management to protect the assets of the organization.

C) The process of mapping external requirements to internal standards.

D) The duty to establish a compliance program within an organization.

54. What are the two important sections of the Sarbanes–Oxley Act (SOX) that have a meaningful impact on public companies and auditors?

A) Sections 401 and 402

B) Sections 302 and 404

C) Sections 201 and 202

D) Sections 501 and 502

55. Under HIPAA, what are covered healthcare providers required to do with identifiable patient information?

A) Store it in a secure physical location only.

B) Use, disclose, and handle it according to strict privacy and security rules.

C) Transfer it to third parties without restrictions.

D) Encrypt it using a government-specified algorithm.

56. What is the role of the Board of Directors in relation to the information security program addressed in GLBA?

A) They must report program effectiveness to the board.

B) They are responsible for overseeing service provider arrangements.

C) They must audit compliance annually.

D) They are involved in the initial risk assessment process.

57. According to the Federal Sentencing Guidelines, what mandatory action must management show in order to demonstrate "due diligence"?

A) Appoint a high-level manager to oversee compliance with policies.

B) Establish policies, standards, and procedures to guide the workforce.

C) Report program effectiveness annually to the Board.

D) Enforce policies through consistent disciplinary measures.

58. Which act made trade secret theft a federal crime?

A) The Economic Espionage Act of 1996

B) The Foreign Corrupt Practices Act (FCPA)

C) The Sarbanes-Oxley Act (SOX)

D) The Gramm-Leach-Bliley Act (GLBA)

59. What is the 'duty of care' as defined under the "Model Business Corporation Act"?

A) The duty to establish and maintain an effective compliance program.

B) The duty to report on internal controls effectiveness.

C) The duty to discharge responsibilities in good faith and with the care an ordinarily prudent person would exercise.

D) The duty to act in the best interest of all parties when presented with a conflict of interest.

60. What is required by California's SB 1386 law in the event of a compromise involving personal information?

A) Immediate reporting to the Office of the President.

B) Notification of the individuals whose information may have been compromised.

C) A fine of up to $11 million per incident.

D) A credit freeze on the victim's credit report.

61. What primary roles does an information security policy perform?

A) Risk assessment and mitigation

B) Internal guidance and external communication

C) Employee discipline and audit compliance

D) Incident response and system recovery

62. What are the three essential elements that security and privacy policies and procedures must have to be effective?

A) Enforcement, automation, and flexibility

B) Documentation, communication, and currency

C) Redundancy, scalability, and accessibility

D) Authentication, authorization, and accounting

63. What are the three types of policies used in an information security program?

A) Global, Topic-specific, and User-specific

B) Tier 1, Tier 2, and Tier 3

C) Strategic, Operational, and Tactical

D) Organizational, Departmental, and Individual

64. Who is typically responsible for issuing global policies (Tier 1)?

A) IT department

B) Senior management

C) Security administrators

D) All employees

65. What usually triggers the need to create or revise topic-specific policies (Tier 2)?

A) Annual security audits

B) Changes in management

C) Relevant changes in technology or law

D) Quarterly financial reports

66. Which section of a policy typically identifies the consequences for non-compliance?

A) Scope

B) Responsibilities

C) Compliance or Consequences

D) Relevance

67. Where are application-specific policies (Tier 3) typically applied?

A) Throughout the entire enterprise

B) Only within the IT department

C) To individual systems or applications

D) Exclusively at the executive level

68. How should a policy identify the appropriate contacts for further information?

A) By individual name

B) By job title

C) By department only

D) No contact information is needed

69. In what format are policies generally written?

A) Multi-page reports

B) One-page text using both sides of the paper

C) Detailed procedures and flowcharts

D) Extensive legal documents

70. What is the importance of having a policy appear as other published policies from the organization?

A) To ensure legal compliance

B) To improve the document's aesthetics

C) To facilitate reading and critique by members of the review panel

D) To reduce printing costs

71. When developing procedures, what is the recommended way to gather information from Subject Matter Experts (SMEs)?

A) Have the SMEs write the procedures themselves.

B) Develop the procedures without consulting the SMEs.

C) Use a technical writer to interview the SMEs and collect information.

D) Create the procedures solely based on existing documentation.

72. How long should the interview with the SME be scheduled for when gathering information for procedure writing?

A) 30 minutes

B) 45 minutes

C) 60 minutes

D) 90 minutes

73. Why is it not effective to have teams develop procedures?

A) Teams lack the necessary expertise.

B) It is too time-consuming and slows the process down.

C) Teams are not required to approve procedures.

D) Individual experts are more efficient than teams.

74. What should be done after gathering all the necessary information from the SME for procedure writing?

A) The information should be discarded.

B) The information should be put into procedure format.

C) The information should be immediately published.

D) The information should be reviewed by the management team.

75. Who should review the draft procedure for content editing?

A) The management team

B) The technical writer

C) The SME

D) A third-party auditor

76. What is the final step before publishing a procedure?

A) Review the procedure annually.

B) Have the technical writer approve the procedure.

C) Test the procedure to ensure it provides proper results.

D) Have the management team sign off on the procedure.

77. How often should the procedure be reviewed after it has been published?

A) Monthly

B) Quarterly

C) Biannually

D) Annually

78. Who should be informed about the next steps after the interview with the SME?

A) The technical writer only

B) The SME and the SME backup

C) The management team

D) All employees

79. What role does the SME backup play in the procedure writing process?

A) They write the initial draft of the procedure.

B) They provide additional updates to the procedure.

C) They review the updated procedure for a final review.

D) They test the procedure with the SME.

80. Are management teams required to approve procedures?

A) Yes, they are essential for approval.

B) No, teams are not required to approve procedures.

C) Yes, but only in certain organizations.

D) No, but they must be consulted during the approval process.

81. What is the primary purpose of developing a business case for information security program investments?

A) To comply with regulatory requirements.

B) To support annual report figures.

C) To justify funding based on the project's value.

D) To ensure adherence to security protocols.

82. Which of the following is NOT listed as a factor affecting the reliability of ROI as an indicator of corporate value?

A) Length of project life.

B) Company's market share.

C) The capitalization policy.

D) The growth rate of new investment.

83. What does the acronym TCO stand for, and what does it represent?

A) Total Capital Outlay, the complete expense of a capital investment.

B) Total Cost of Ownership, the overall cost of acquiring and maintaining an asset.

C) Technical Cost of Operations, the technical expenses related to operating a system.

D) Total Cost of Operations, the total cost related to the usage and maintenance of a system.

84. What does the ROSI formula calculate?

A) The cost per year to recover from intrusions.

B) The annual benefit divided by the investment amount.

C) The economic value of a security investment.

D) The dollar savings from preventing intrusions.

85. According to the text, what are some examples of indirect costs included in TCO?

A) Employee salaries and office rent.

B) Costs of failure or outage and costs of security breaches.

C) Purchase cost of equipment and installation fees.

D) Depreciation rates and capitalization policies.

86. What is the significance of research groups at universities like Idaho, MIT, and Carnegie Mellon developing ROSI calculations?

A) They provide standardized security protocols for organizations.

B) They have created a new regulatory framework for information security.

C) They offer robust and supportable data to integrate into business case models.

D) They are replacing the traditional ROI calculations with ROSI.

87. What is the primary benefit of advancements in single sign-on and user access provisioning technologies, according to the text?

A) They provide better security for enterprise systems.

B) They result in savings in time and cost over traditional manual administration techniques.

C) They increase the ROI of security investments.

D) They help in meeting compliance regulations more efficiently.

88. What are the components of the ROSI formula as mentioned?

A) (R-E) + T = ALE

B) TCO = DC + IC

C) ROI = Annual Benefit / Investment Amount

D) R – (ALE) = ROSI

89. Why is the ROI formula considered unreliable for determining an information security program's success or corporate value?

A) Because it does not consider the cost of capital.

B) Because it overstates the economic value based on certain factors.

C) Because it only calculates the direct costs involved.

D) Because it is only applicable to non-security related investments.

90. What are the two financial metrics that are commonly used to justify spending on projects?

A) Cost-Benefit Analysis (CBA) and Economic Value Added (EVA).

B) Net Present Value (NPV) and Internal Rate of Return (IRR).

C) Return on Investment (ROI) and Total Cost of Ownership (TCO).

D) Gross Profit Margin (GPM) and Operating Profit Margin (OPM).

91. What is the primary goal of risk management in a business context?

A) To increase operational costs.

B) To identify, control, and minimize the impact of uncertain events.

C) To eliminate all business risks.

D) To focus solely on financial gains.

92. What does risk analysis help to define?

A) Preventive measures for reducing the probability of risks.

B) The total profit of a project.

C) The roles and responsibilities within a team.

D) The marketing strategy for a business.

93. What is the formula represented in the text for computing a single instance of risk within a system?

A) Asset + Threat + Vulnerability

B) Asset / Threat / Vulnerability

C) Asset * Threat * Vulnerability

D) Asset - Threat - Vulnerability

94. What is the purpose of vulnerability assessment and controls evaluation?

A) To measure the profitability of a company's product.

B) To determine the adequacy of security measures and identify security deficiencies.

C) To compute the total cost of IT infrastructure.

D) To evaluate the performance of employees.

95. What is the computation of risk known as?

A) Risk Mitigation

B) Risk Analysis

C) Risk Assessment

D) Vulnerability Assessment

96. Which process involves implementing controls to prevent identified risks from occurring?

A) Risk Analysis

B) Risk Assessment

C) Risk Mitigation

D) Risk Management

97. Who is considered the functional owner of an enterprise's assets, according to the text?

A) The risk manager.

B) Senior management of a department or business unit.

C) The shareholders of the company.

D) The IT department.

98. What must senior management ensure regarding the enterprise they manage?

A) That it follows all the government regulations.

B) That it has the capabilities needed to accomplish its mission or business objectives.

C) That it maximizes shareholder wealth.

D) That all employees are satisfied.

99. What demonstrates senior management's due diligence in the context of risk management?

A) Increasing the company's market share.

B) Support of the risk management process.

C) Outperforming competitors financially.

D) Cutting operational costs.

100. What does the total risk for a network equate to?

A) The sum of all profits.

B) The sum of all risk instances.

C) The sum of all assets.

D) The sum of all vulnerabilities.

101. What is the primary purpose of conducting a risk analysis, according to the text?

A) To comply with audit requirements

B) To document due diligence in the decision-making process

C) To establish an IT process within the company

D) To create an information classification policy

102. According to the SDLC phases outlined, where does the actual creation or implementation of the system or process take place?

A) Analysis Phase

B) Design Phase

C) Construction Phase

D) Test Phase

103. What role is responsible for the organization's planning, budgeting, and performance, including its information security components?

A) Senior Management

B) Chief Information Security Officer (CISO)

C) Resource Owners

D) Information Security Professional

104. What is the first phase of the typical System Development Life Cycle (SDLC) as used by the National Institute of Standards and Technology (NIST)?

A) Initiation

B) Development or Acquisition

C) Implementation

D) Operation or Maintenance

105. What is the role of 'Resource Owners' in the context of risk management?

A) They are responsible for IT security only.

B) They make decisions on business objectives and missions.

C) They ensure proper controls are in place for the information resources they own.

D) They conduct the Network Vulnerability Assessment (NVA).

106. What should be conducted to determine if implemented controls or safeguards are effective?

A) Risk Analysis

B) Risk Assessment

C) Network Vulnerability Assessment (NVA)

D) Business Impact Analysis (BIA)

107. What is the correct order of phases in the SDLC as outlined by the National Institute of Standards and Technology (NIST)?

A) Initiation, Implementation, Development or Acquisition, Operation or Maintenance, Disposal

B) Initiation, Development or Acquisition, Implementation, Operation or Maintenance, Disposal

C) Development or Acquisition, Initiation, Implementation, Operation or Maintenance, Disposal

D) Operation or Maintenance, Initiation, Development or Acquisition, Implementation, Disposal

108. When should a risk analysis be conducted, according to the text?

A) After a project is completed

B) Before starting a task, project, or development cycle

C) At the end of each financial year

D) When a security breach occurs

109. In the context of information security, what does the term 'vulnerability' refers to?

A) A well-secured network system

B) A condition of a missing or ineffectively administered safeguard or control

C) A risk that cannot be mitigated

D) A threat that has already caused damage

110. What is the term used to describe the person responsible for the organization's security programs, including risk management?

A) Senior Management

B) Chief Information Security Officer (CISO)

C) Information Security Professional

D) Resource Owner

111. What is the primary objective of conducting a risk identification and analysis in a project?

A) To ensure the project is completed on time

B) To guarantee the success of the project with no risks

C) To identify and assess factors that may jeopardize the success of a project

D) To assign tasks to project team members

112. In the context of risk analysis, why is it important to consider the cost of not moving forward with a project?

A) To ensure that all possible expenses are billed to the client

B) To comply with regulatory compliance issues

C) To understand the impact of the decision on the enterprise's competitive advantage

D) To simplify the project management process

113. What are some of the costs that must be factored into a project's risk analysis?

A) Procurement or development, operation, and maintenance costs

B) Only the costs of final product delivery to the customer

C) Costs associated with staff entertainment and perks

D) Solely the costs of marketing and advertising the project

114. What is a key deliverable from the asset definition step in the risk assessment process?

A) A detailed marketing plan

B) A risk assessment statement of opportunity

C) A full financial audit of the enterprise

D) A complete inventory of organizational assets

115. During the risk assessment process, what is the purpose of threat identification?

A) To train employees on cybersecurity

B) To determine the project's budget

C) To create a list of potential threat sources that could affect the business objectives

D) To establish a new company policy

116. Which of the following is NOT a major category of threat-sources identified in the risk assessment process?

A) Natural threats

B) Human threats

C) Environmental threats

D) Astrological threats

117. What is the correct sequence of steps in the risk assessment process?

A) Asset Definition, Threat Identification, Determine Probability of Occurrence, Determine the Impact of the Threat, Controls Recommended, Documentation

B) Threat Identification, Determine the Impact of the Threat, Asset Definition, Controls Recommended, Determine Probability of Occurrence, Documentation

C) Threat Identification, Asset Definition, Documentation, Determine Probability of Occurrence, Determine the Impact of the Threat, Controls Recommended

D) Documentation, Asset Definition, Determine Probability of Occurrence, Determine the Impact of the Threat, Threat Identification, Controls Recommended

118. What should be considered when performing a cost-benefit analysis for new or enhanced controls?

A) The popularity of the control among employees

B) The aesthetic appeal of the control

C) The cost of implementation and maintenance of the control

D) The opinion of external consultants only

119. Which of the following is NOT a method of risk mitigation discussed in the text?

A) Risk Assumption

B) Risk Augmentation

C) Risk Transference

D) Risk Avoidance

120. What does the term 'Risk Level' refer to in the context of risk assessment?

A) The salary level of the risk assessment team lead

B) The number of risks identified in a project

C) The function of the probability that an identified threat will occur and the impact it will have

D) The size of the team conducting the risk assessment

121. What is the primary goal of an effective risk assessment process in relation to an enterprise's business objectives?

A) To enforce strict security and audit requirements

B) To ensure that all risks are completely eliminated

C) To identify safeguards that meet the business needs of the enterprise

D) To mandate compliance with all industry regulations

122. Which top IS project managers identified functional capability as the most needed for success?

A) Cost Management

B) Technical Expertise

C) Risk Management

D) Interpersonal Communication

123. What are the three common sources of threats that should be considered during a risk assessment?

A) Natural, accidental, and competitive

B) Internal, external, and strategic

C) Natural, human, and environmental

D) Logical, physical, and procedural

124. What are the three elements of the information security triad that are focused on during the risk assessment process?

A) Usability, efficiency, and reliability

B) Integrity, confidentiality, and availability

C) Authentication, authorization, and accounting

D) Encryption, firewall, and antivirus

125. Which method did the text mention for establishing the likelihood of a threat occurrence when calculating Annual Loss Exposure (ALE)?

A) Qualitative risk assessment

B) Threat source table

C) Threat occurrence rate table

D) Asset value estimation

126. Which of the following is NOT a recommended consideration when selecting controls and safeguards during the risk assessment process?

A) The effectiveness of the control

B) The popularity of the control in the industry

C) Legal and regulatory requirements for specific controls

D) The operational impact of the control on the organization

127. What is the process that must remain with the business unit and cannot be discharged to third parties, according to the text?

A) Implementing encryption techniques

B) Conducting annual security training

C) Establishing information classification policy

D) Outsourcing security operations

128. What is the first step in the risk assessment process described in the text?

A) Threat Identification

B) Asset Identification

C) Risk Level Establishment

D) Control Selection

129. In the context of information security, what does 'Loss of Integrity' refer to?

A) The inability to access critical systems

B) Unauthorized changes made to data or the system

C) Disclosure of confidential information

D) Physical theft of enterprise property

130. What is the risk assessment team advised to do once threats have been identified and consolidated?

A) Disregard low-level threats

B) Establish a risk level for each threat

C) Immediately implement countermeasures

D) Conduct a detailed financial analysis

131. What is one of the primary roles of an information security manager regarding risk?

A) To create a yearly financial report

B) To update the risk assessment only when there is a security breach

C) To report significant changes in risk to management on a periodic and event-driven basis

D) To focus solely on technical aspects of security

132. When should the risk assessment used by the information security manager be updated?

A) Only when there is a change in management

B) Annually, as a standard procedure

C) As changes occur within the organization

D) When the information security manager deems it necessary

133. What should be included in the periodic update meetings with upper management?

A) Personal achievements of the security team

B) Updates on IT equipment purchases

C) The status of the organization's overall security program

D) Details of every minor security incident

134. What should trigger a special report to upper management?

A) Any change in the security team

B) Routine software updates

C) A significant security breach or security event

D) Minor changes in risk assessment

135. What is the disadvantage of quantitative risk assessment?

A) Calculations are simple

B) Results can be expressed in management-specific language

C) Calculations are complex

D) It involves non-security and non-technical staff

136. What is an advantage of qualitative risk assessment?

A) It requires determining the monetary value of assets

B) Cost/benefit assessment effort is essential

C) Easier to involve non-security and non-technical staff

D) It provides objective processes and metrics

137. What is the disadvantage of qualitative risk assessment?

A) Calculations are simple

B) It is very subjective in nature

C) Not necessary to quantify threat frequency

D) Provides flexibility in process and reporting

138. How should sensitive information be communicated when reporting to upper management?

A) Through public channels for transparency

B) Using a secure channel

C) In person at social events

D) Via company-wide email

139. Why is it not necessary to determine the dollar value of an asset in qualitative risk assessment?

A) Because all assets are considered equally valuable

B) Because it is assumed that all assets have no monetary value

C) Because qualitative assessment does not focus on cost

D) Because qualitative assessment is not based on monetary value but on subjective analysis

140. What should an information security manager define regarding significant security events?

A) The entertainment for the annual security gala

B) Processes for evaluating the events based on their impact on the organization

C) The color code for security clearances

D) The brand of security hardware to be used

141. What is the main purpose of conducting a gap analysis in information security management?

A) To assess the performance of employees

B) To evaluate financial risks

C) To measure the maturity level of the security program

D) To calculate the company's annual profit

142. When establishing Recovery Time Objectives (RTO), what analysis must an organization conduct?

A) Competitor Analysis

B) Business Impact Analysis (BIA)

C) SWOT Analysis

D) Market Analysis

143. What are the four essential aspects of information classification?

A) Cost, Quality, Quantity, and Time

B) Legal standpoint, Responsibility, Integrity, and Criticality

C) Storage, Transmission, Usage, and Archiving

D) Confidentiality, Integrity, Availability, and Non-repudiation

144. Which statement best represents the old concept in computer security regarding information access?

A) Information is open until it requires closing.

B) All information is of equal value.

C) Everything is closed until it is opened.

D) All enterprise information needs employee access.

145. How many information classification categories does the text suggest are typically sufficient for an organization's needs?

A) One or two

B) Three or four

C) Five or six

D) Seven or more

146. What is a potential problem with classifying all information as 'confidential'?

A) It simplifies the classification process.

B) It may violate the concept of placing controls where needed.

C) It decreases the overall security of the information.

D) It requires less resources to manage.

147. Why should organizations avoid directly adopting classification categories from another enterprise?

A) Because all organizations have identical information

B) Because it undermines the value of the information

C) Because each organization's needs and definitions are unique

D) Because it is prohibited by ISO 17799

148. What should be done with classified information once it no longer meets the criteria for its classification?

A) It should be kept indefinitely for historical records.

B) It should be automatically downgraded or declassified.

C) It should be transferred to a competitor.

D) It should be published publicly.

149. What is one part of an effective information classification program?

A) Increasing the number of copies of documents

B) Destroying documents when they are no longer required

C) Classifying all documents as confidential

D) Ensuring all employees have access to classified documents

150. What does information classification help to establish in terms of protection control requirements?

A) The need for universal access to information

B) A baseline for employee performance reviews

C) Protection levels commensurate with information value

D) The requirement for all information to be encrypted

151. Which OSI layer is responsible for physically transmitting data over the communication link?

A) Application Layer

B) Network Layer

C) Transport Layer

D) Physical Layer

152. What type of information is sent at the Data Link Layer of the OSI model?

A) Bits

B) Packets

C) Frames

D) Segments

153. Which OSI layer provides administratively assigned addresses?

A) Data Link Layer

B) Network Layer

C) Session Layer

D) Application Layer

154. Which protocol is an example of a Network Layer protocol?

A) Transmission Control Protocol (TCP)

B) User Datagram Protocol (UDP)

C) Internet Protocol (IP)

D) Hypertext Transfer Protocol (HTTP)

155. What is the function of the Transport Layer?

A) Routing of information

B) Flow control

C) Formatting data representation

D) Organizing interaction between applications

156. Which of the following devices operates at the Data Link Layer?

A) Hubs

B) Switches

C) Routers

D) Proxies

157. What is the primary function of the Session Layer?

A) Data transfer

B) Structuring interaction between applications

C) Data format translation

D) Accessing lower OSI functions

158. What is the purpose of the Application Layer in the OSI model?

A) Handling the peculiarities of the actual transfer medium

B) Error detection and correction

C) Supporting semantic exchanges between applications

D) Representing user or system data

159. What is the risk associated with using DHCP in a network?

A) Data sequencing issues

B) Unauthorized access to network addresses

C) Overloading the network with static IP addresses

D) Incorrect data format translation

160. At which OSI layer would you find error correction as a responsibility?

A) Physical Layer

B) Data Link Layer

C) Transport Layer

D) Presentation Layer

161. What is the primary purpose of the Transmission Control Protocol/Internet Protocol (TCP/IP) model?

A) To define data compression methods

B) To serve as the foundation and framework for many computer networks

C) To allocate unique IP addresses to each computer

D) To document the fundamental truths of networking

162. How many layers does the TCP/IP model have?

A) Two

B) Four

C) Seven

D) Twelve

163. Which RFC is known for describing the encapsulation of IP datagrams on avian carriers?

A) RFC 1149

B) RFC 1925

C) RFC 2324

D) RFC 2549

164. What does a subnet mask in IP networking determine?

A) The total number of available IP addresses

B) The division of network and host parts of an IP address

C) The type of error checking to be used

D) The data compression method to be used

165. What is the first-byte range for a Class A network?

A) 1-126

B) 128-191

C) 192-223

D) 224-255

166. How many hosts can a Class B network approximately have?

A) 256

B) 17 million

C) 65,000

D) Unlimited

167. Which RFC provides a humorous take on a protocol suite involving monkeys?

A) RFC 793

B) RFC 2795

C) RFC 1918

D) RFC 768

168. Which of the following is NOT an actual RFC related to information security?

A) RFC 768: User Datagram Protocol (UDP)

B) RFC 2324: Hypertext Coffee Pot Control Protocol (HTCPCP/1.0)

C) RFC 1149: A Standard for the Transmission of IP Datagrams on Avian Carriers

D) RFC 1918: Address Allocation for Private Intranets (IP)

169. What is the correct order of layers in the TCP/IP model from top to bottom?

A) Network Interface, Internet, Host to Host, Application

B) Host to Host, Internet, Network Interface, Application

C) Application, Host to Host, Internet, Network Interface

D) Application, Internet, Network Interface, Host to Host

170. Which class of IP addresses is used specifically for multicast traffic?

A) Class A

B) Class B

C) Class C

D) Class D

171. What is the purpose of the Time to Live (TTL) field in an IP datagram header?

A) To specify the transport protocol of the segment.

B) To ensure datagrams do not travel forever if a network path contains a loop.

C) To indicate the position of a fragment relative to the starting fragment.

D) To specify how long a datagram can remain on the network based on distance.

172. Which of the following is NOT a reason to use Network Address Translation (NAT)?

A) To conserve Internet available (public) IP addresses.

B) To provide security by hiding the organization's internal IP addresses.

C) To increase the speed of the Internet connection.

D) To allow private IP addresses to communicate with the Internet.

173. Which address range is referred to as the "24-bit block" of private IP addresses?

A) 10.0.0.0–10.255.255.255

B) 172.16.0.0–172.31.255.255

C) 192.168.0.0–192.168.255.255

D) 203.49.27.136–203.49.27.255

174. What is the main function of the Header Checksum field in the IP datagram header?

A) To provide a unique identification for each datagram.

B) To protect the header against errors during transmission.

C) To indicate the length of the IP datagram header.

D) To determine the data payload size.

175. Which IP address would be considered a public IP address?

A) 10.1.1.1

B) 172.16.0.1

C) 192.168.1.1

D) 203.49.27.136

176. How many contiguous class C network numbers are present in the "16-bit block" of private IP addresses?

A) 16

B) 256

C) 1024

D) 2048

177. What is the purpose of the Fragment Offset field in the IP datagram header?

A) To identify the transport layer protocol.

B) To define the entire datagram size.

C) To specify the position of a fragment in a fragmented datagram.

D) To list options used for routing and time-stamping.

178. What does the Protocol field in the IP datagram header indicate?

A) The total length of the IP datagram.

B) The upper layer protocol to which the data portion of the datagram should be passed.

C) The version of the IP datagram.

D) The length of the datagram's header.

179. Which of the following devices is NOT typically used to perform Network Address Translation (NAT)?

A) Firewalls

B) Layer three switches

C) Cable/DSL modems

D) Network Attached Storage (NAS)

180. Which IP address ranges are reserved for Category 1 hosts that do not require access to the Internet at large?

A) 10.0.0.0–10.255.255.255

B) 172.16.0.0–172.31.255.255

C) 192.168.0.0–192.168.255.255

D) All of the above

181. What is the primary role of the Transmission Control Protocol (TCP) in network communications?

A) To provide a connectionless datagram service

B) To provide a connection-oriented, stateful protocol for reliable communication

C) To assign IP addresses to devices on a network

D) To encrypt data for secure transmission over a network

182. Which range of port numbers is known as the 'well-known' ports?

A) 0 to 255

B) 0 to 1023

C) 1024 to 49151

D) 49152 to 65535

183. Which port number is commonly used for HTTP traffic?

A) 21

B) 53

C) 80

D) 443

184. What is the purpose of a port in computer networking?

A) To connect multiple computers in a local network

B) To provide a specific memory address space for running services

C) To encrypt data packets for security

D) To assign IP addresses to devices

185. What is the main difference between TCP and UDP port numbers?

A) TCP port numbers are always even, while UDP port numbers are always odd.

B) TCP port numbers are used exclusively for secure transmissions, while UDP port numbers are not.

C) TCP and UDP have separate memory address spaces for their ports.

D) UDP port numbers can only be used for local network communications.

186. What does a closed port response during a port scan indicate?

A) The port is actively accepting connections.

B) The port is open but not actively listening for connections.

C) The port responds indicating it is not open for connections.

D) A firewall is blocking the port scan request.

187. Which flag in the TCP header is used to start communication between systems by synchronizing sequence numbers?

A) URG

B) ACK

C) SYN

D) FIN

188. In the TCP header, what is the purpose of the Window field?

A) To specify the sequence number of the octet following the urgent data.

B) To indicate the size of the largest segment the sender wishes to receive.

C) To tell the source how fast to send the packets and manage data flow.

D) To add bits to the TCP header to ensure it is a multiple of 32 bits.

189. What is one of the common responses a port may have to a port scan?

A) Active

B) Dynamic

C) Filtered

D) Random

190. Which TCP header field is used to check for errors in the TCP header and parts of the IP header?

A) Urgent Pointer

B) Checksum

C) Options

D) Padding

191. What is the main function of the SYN flag in a TCP three-way handshake?

A) To terminate the connection

B) To acknowledge the receipt of a packet

C) To synchronize sequence numbers

D) To indicate an error in the connection

192. What is the purpose of using a pseudorandom Initial Sequence Number (ISN) in TCP connections?

A) To improve connection speed

B) To make the ISN easy to predict

C) To ensure the reliability of data transmission

D) To avoid sequence number conflicts and security risks

193. Which packet does Bob send to Sally in response to her SYN packet during the three-way handshake?

A) ACK packet

B) FIN packet

C) SYN packet

D) SYN-ACK packet

194. What is the role of the ACK packet in the TCP three-way handshake?

A) To start a TCP connection

B) To acknowledge the receipt of the SYN-ACK packet

C) To synchronize sequence numbers

D) To terminate the TCP connection

195. Which of the following best describes the TCP three-way handshake process?

A) SYN-ACK, SYN, ACK

B) SYN, SYN-ACK, ACK

C) SYN, ACK, SYN-ACK

D) ACK, SYN, SYN-ACK

196. How does the TCP protocol ensure that a new connection's ISN does not conflict with a previous one?

A) By always starting with a sequence number of 1

B) By using a fixed sequence number

C) By using a timed counter and pseudorandom algorithms

D) By waiting for the previous connection to time out

197. Which flag does Sally set to terminate the TCP connection with Bob?

A) ACK

B) SYN

C) FIN

D) RST

198. What type of protocol is UDP when compared to TCP?

A) Connection-oriented

B) Connectionless

C) Stateful

D) Synchronous

199. Why might an application choose to use UDP over TCP?

A) To ensure data reliability

B) To provide connection-based communication

C) For speed and low overhead in data transfer

D) To use sequence numbers and acknowledgments

200. How does UDP respond to a packet addressed to a port that is not open?

A) By sending a SYN packet

B) By sending an ICMP error message

C) By initiating a three-way handshake

D) By sending a RST packet

201. What is the primary goal of the ICMP protocol?

A) To encrypt data

B) To transport data

C) To troubleshoot networks

D) To authenticate users

202. Which OSI layer does ICMP operate at?

A) Application Layer

B) Transport Layer

C) Network Layer

D) Presentation Layer

203. What is the length of the Type field in the ICMP header?

A) 16 bits

B) 8 bits

C) 32 bits

D) 4 bits

204. What does a Code value of 0 signify in a Type 3 ICMP message?

A) Host Unreachable

B) Network Unreachable

C) Protocol Unreachable

D) Port Unreachable

205. Which ICMP Type corresponds to an echo request?

A) Type 0

B) Type 3

C) Type 8

D) Type 11

206. What is the purpose of the checksum field in ICMP packets?

A) To encrypt data

B) To check the integrity of the header

C) To store the packet sequence number

D) To identify the next-hop router

207. What is the typical content of the data portion of an ICMP packet?

A) The original message data

B) Random characters

C) The IP header and first 64 bits of the original packet

D) A copy of the ICMP header

208. Which ICMP message type indicates that a router cannot forward a packet onto the next hop?

A) Type 4

B) Type 3

C) Type 11

D) Type 0

209. What diagnostic tool uses ICMP messages to determine the path to a destination?

A) Ping

B) Trace route

C) Netstat

D) Nslookup

210. What are the risks associated with IP protocols like ICMP in terms of security?

A) They are too complex to configure

B) They prioritize speed over security

C) They were designed with strong security in mind

D) They were not designed with security as a priority

211. What is the primary goal of information security according to the CIA Triad?

A) To ensure system performance under heavy utilization

B) To safeguard the company's financial assets

C) To protect the accuracy, confidentiality, and availability of information

D) To prevent any external threats using firewalls

212. According to ISO 17799, what does 'integrity' mean in the context of information security?

A) The action of ensuring information is accessible only to authorized users

B) The action of safeguarding the accuracy and completeness of information and processing methods

C) The action of maintaining authorized user access to information and associated assets when required

D) The action of keeping secret information confidential

213. What does RAID stand for, according to linux.org?

A) Rapid Array of Independent Disks

B) Redundant Array of Inexpensive Disks

C) Reliable Array of Integrated Disks

D) Resilient Array of Interconnected Disks

214. Which RAID level combines the techniques of mirroring and striping?

A) RAID 0

B) RAID 1

C) RAID 5

D) RAID 10

215. What is the primary purpose of a UPS in information security?

A) To detect and remove viruses from the system

B) To balance the load across multiple servers

C) To maintain the availability of a system during a power failure

D) To provide additional storage capacity for data backup

216. What is the PPPN model used by ISACA in the CISM certification?

A) Process, Physical, Platform, Network

B) Policy, Procedure, Protection, Network

C) Process, Policy, Plan, Network

D) Physical, Platform, Protection, Node

217. Which control would be classified as a 'Platform' control?

A) Firewalls

B) Visitor badges

C) Operating system security controls

D) Intrusion detection systems

218. Which of the following is an example of a 'Process' control within the PPPN model?

A) RAID configurations

B) Virus detection software

C) Security policies and procedures

D) Biometric access systems

219. What is the disadvantage of using RAID systems in terms of storage space?

A) The total storage space is less than the sum of individual drives.

B) RAID systems require additional drives for system performance.

C) They increase the risk of data loss due to multiple drive failures.

D) RAID systems do not support modern solid-state drives.

220. What is the function of system failover technology?

A) To maintain data integrity by preventing unauthorized access

B) To ensure data confidentiality by encrypting information

C) To balance the load during high network traffic

D) To switch to a secondary system in case the primary system fails

221. What is the primary goal of a cracker when breaking into a system?

A) To improve security of the system

B) To explore and notify the system administrator

C) To cause as much damage as possible

D) To perform a routine check for vulnerabilities

222. What is a common way for attackers to maintain access after compromising a server?

A) Resetting the server

B) Deleting system files

C) Uploading custom applications or backdoors

D) Changing passwords

223. Which phase of the attacking methodology involves removing traces of the attacker's presence from the system logs?

A) Reconnaissance

B) Scanning

C) Gaining Access

D) Covering Tracks

224. What type of malicious code disguises itself as a legitimate program but performs malicious actions without the user's knowledge?

A) Virus

B) Worm

C) Trojan horse

D) Logic bomb

225. What is a logic bomb designed to do?

A) Infect files like a virus

B) Replicate itself across networks

C) Execute when a specific condition is met

D) Appear as a legitimate program

226. Which of the following is NOT a characteristic of a Distributed Denial-of-Service (DDoS) attack?

A) It involves a single attacker machine.

B) It utilizes zombie hosts.

C) It can flood telecommunications lines.

D) It may use tools like Trinoo or TFN2K.

227. What is the first phase in the basic hacker methodology?

A) Gaining Access

B) Reconnaissance

C) Scanning

D) Maintaining Access

228. What does a rootkit allow an attacker to do?

A) Infect the system with a virus

B) Send spam emails

C) Replace system files with Trojans

D) Perform a denial-of-service attack

229. What is the main difference between a virus and a worm?

A) A virus is harmless, while a worm is malicious.

B) A virus replicates by attaching to other files, while a worm is standalone.

C) A virus does not require user interaction to spread, while a worm does.

D) A virus can only infect one computer, while a worm spreads through networks.

230. Which type of attack is designed to overwhelm a target's hardware resources or telecommunication lines?

A) Phishing attack

B) Man-in-the-middle attack

C) Denial-of-Service (DoS) attack

D) SQL injection attack

231. What is the primary goal of social engineering attacks?

A) To improve system security

B) To trick individuals into revealing sensitive information

C) To physically break into secure locations

D) To provide technical support to users

232. Which of the following is NOT a quality that social engineers exploit?

A) The desire to be helpful

B) A tendency to trust people

C) The fear of getting into trouble

D) An inclination to follow strict security procedures

233. What is a 'dictionary attack'?

A) A method that involves guessing passwords through a random generation of characters

B) An attack that physically damages dictionaries to prevent language-based encryption

C) An attack using a list of common passwords to guess credentials quickly

D) A social engineering tactic involving the manipulation of language

234. What is the difference between a brute force attack and a dictionary attack?

A) A brute force attack is less time-consuming

B) A dictionary attack tries every possible combination of characters

C) A brute force attack uses a pre-determined list of common passwords

D) A dictionary attack is often successful due to users choosing simple passwords

235. What is a Man-in-the-Middle (MITM) attack?

A) An attack where the hacker physically stands between two communicating parties

B) A social engineering technique where the attacker pretends to be an intermediary

C) An attack where the hacker inserts themselves into a communication process to intercept data

D) A brute force attack on network communications

236. What is the focus of Mandatory Access Control (MAC)?

A) To provide access based on users' job functions

B) To assign permissions based on a defined policy

C) To allow data owners to assign ownership of data to others

D) To create a flexible access environment for rapidly changing organizations

237. Which access control model is characterized by flexibility and less administrative overhead?

A) MAC

B) DAC

C) Firewall-based access control

D) Intrusion Detection System (IDS)-based access control

238. Why might an organization choose to implement Discretionary Access Control (DAC) over Mandatory Access Control (MAC)?

A) DAC is typically more secure than MAC

B) DAC is more suitable for organizations requiring the highest security standards

C) DAC is less expensive and more flexible than MAC

D) DAC requires a written policy for access control for the entire organization

239. What is the main disadvantage of using Discretionary Access Control (DAC)?

A) It is more costly than MAC

B) It is less flexible than MAC

C) It can lead to security breaches over time due to its flexibility

D) It requires every document to be classified

240. Which of the following is an advantage of Mandatory Access Control (MAC)?

A) Lower cost than DAC

B) Greater flexibility in rapidly changing environments

C) Ability for data owners to assign ownership of data

D) Generally provides greater security than DAC

241. What is the primary goal of access control?

A) To ensure user convenience

B) To create nonrepudiation with a userID-password combination

C) To enforce password changes regularly

D) To provide the easiest password selection standard

242. What type of authentication method is based on something the user knows?

A) Biometrics

B) Tokens

C) Passwords or PINs

D) Voiceprint systems

243. Which access control system allows an information security manager to view security violations and where additional security needs to be implemented?

A) Role-Based Access Control (RBAC)

B) Lattice-Based Access Control

C) Rule-Based Access Control

D) Access Control Lists

244. What is the major drawback to script-based Single Sign-On (SSO)?

A) It is easily hacked.

B) It is expensive to implement.

C) Passwords are stored and transmitted in plaintext.

D) It is no longer used in modern systems.

245. What is a characteristic of Role-Based Access Control (RBAC)?

A) It assigns permissions to individual users.

B) Permissions are assigned to job functions rather than users.

C) It is primarily used for low turnover job roles.

D) It increases administration overhead.

246. Which of the following is a benefit of token-based authentication?

A) It is an inexpensive solution.

B) Tokens are difficult to lose.

C) It introduces complexity to the authentication process.

D) It is based on biometrics.

247. What are the three methods by which a user can authenticate to access control systems?

A) Username, password, and biometrics

B) Knowledge-based, characteristics-based, and possession-based

C) Password, token, and two-factor authentication

D) PIN, token, and voice recognition

248. What does two-factor authentication require?

A) Two different types of knowledge-based methods

B) A combination of two different categories of authentication methods

C) Two different tokens

D) Two separate passwords

249. What type of attack is mitigated by using one-time passwords?

A) Phishing attacks

B) Network sniffer attacks

C) Denial of Service (DoS) attacks

D) Cross-site scripting (XSS) attacks

250. What is an example of an Access Control List (ACL)?

A) A list of users who have logged into the system

B) A firewall's rules that determine which IP addresses have access

C) A system log that records password changes

D) An organizational chart with employee roles and responsibilities

251. Which protocol is primarily used as the back-end authentication mechanism for 802.1x networks?

A) TACACS+

B) DHCP

C) Diameter

D) RADIUS

252. What is the transport-layer protocol used by RADIUS?

A) TCP

B) HTTP

C) UDP

D) SSL

253. What newer protocol aims to replace RADIUS and uses TCP as its transport-layer protocol?

A) SSH

B) Diameter

C) SSL

D) TACACS+

254. What does the acronym TACACS stand for?

A) Terminal Access Controller Access-Control System

B) Trusted Authentication Configuration Access Control Service

C) Terminal Access Centralized Authentication Control Server

D) Temporary Access Control Application Command Set

255. Which of the following is not a feature provided by 802.1x and EAP?

A) Assignment of a specific IP address to a user

B) Dynamic configuration of the correct Virtual Local Area Network (VLAN)

C) Enforcing a security policy on the entire Internet

D) Loading the appropriate firewall ruleset for a user

256. What is the role of EAP in the context of 802.1x?

A) It is a transport-layer protocol.

B) It provides extensible authentication.

C) It is a firewall policy.

D) It is a web authentication service.

257. What is an example of a physical zone of control?

A) An antivirus software

B) The fourth floor of an office building

C) A user's account information

D) A firewall policy

258. What is the primary purpose of a firewall?

A) To provide backup solutions

B) To encrypt data

C) To enforce security policy by network segmentation

D) To increase network speed

259. When is communication considered inside the zone of control?

A) When the sender is using a secure protocol

B) When the sender or receiver is within the zone

C) When both the sender and the receiver are located within the zone

D) When the communication passes through a firewall

260. What does 802.1x standardize for network authentication in dynamic environments such as educational institutions?

A) Static IP address allocation

B) Extensible authentication through EAP

C) Global internet security policies

D. Hardware-based network features

261. What type of firewall operates at the application layer of the OSI model?

A) Packet Filter Firewalls

B) Stateful Inspection Firewalls

C) Proxy-Based Firewalls

D) VLANs

262. Which firewall technology requires only two rules to allow a corporate client machine to browse a website instead of four in a packet filter firewall?

A) Packet Filter Firewalls

B) Stateful Inspection Firewalls

C) Proxy-Based Firewalls

D) VLANs

263. What is the major security concern with packet filter firewalls?

A) They are slow.

B) They are expensive.

C) They have several open ports.

D) They require complex configurations.

264. Which type of firewall builds a small dynamic database with connection information?

A) Packet Filter Firewalls

B) Stateful Inspection Firewalls

C) Proxy-Based Firewalls

D) VLANs

265. What is a characteristic advantage of packet filter firewalls?

A) They are the most secure firewalls.

B) They are very fast.

C) They support only common applications.

D) They are application-aware.

266. Proxy-based firewalls are NOT well-suited for which type of applications?

A) HTTP

B) FTP

C) Custom Applications

D) E-mail

267. Which type of firewall has a primary disadvantage related to anti-spoofing issues?

A) Packet Filter Firewalls

B) Stateful Inspection Firewalls

C) Proxy-Based Firewalls

D) VLANs

268. What is the main function of VLANs in terms of network security?

A) Filtering packets

B) Monitoring connection states

C) Creating network segmentation/subdomain isolation

D) Inspecting packet content

269. What disadvantages do proxy-based firewalls and stateful inspection firewalls share?

A) They are both slow.

B) They both have open ports issues.

C) They both require extensive client configuration.

D) They both can be expensive.

270. Which type of firewall is often included for free with other network devices, such as low-end modems and routers?

A) Packet Filter Firewalls

B) Stateful Inspection Firewalls

C) Proxy-Based Firewalls

D) VLANs

271. What is the primary disadvantage of using physical distance as a method of segmentation or subdomain isolation?

A) It is extremely complex to implement

B) It has a high cost

C) It offers minimal security

D) It is not a recognized method

272. How can subnetting be used to isolate networks?

A) By using a single IP address range

B) By physically separating network hardware

C) By assigning two different IP address ranges

D) By deploying a firewall

273. What is the main reason why Network-Based Intrusion Detection Systems (NIDS) are becoming less effective?

A) High cost of maintenance

B) Lack of user-friendliness

C) Encryption of network traffic

D) Frequent hardware failures

274. Which of the following is a consequence of an intrusion detection system using anomaly identification and encountering a new application?

A) It will enhance the network performance

B) It may incorrectly identify legitimate traffic as an attack

C) It will automatically update its baseline

D) It will reduce the number of false positives

275. What is a router's role in network segmentation or subdomain isolation?

A) It encrypts data packets

B) It connects different IP address ranges

C) It blocks communication between network segments through an ACL

D) It monitors for intrusion detection

276. What is the most secure method of segmentation or subdomain isolation mentioned in the text?

A) Physical distance

B) Subnetting

C) Routing

D) Firewall

277. What percentage of intrusions are typically conducted by internal employees?

A) 30%

B) 50%

C) 70%

D) 90%

278. What is a significant drawback of automated IDS responses?

A) They are too slow to react

B) They require constant manual intervention

C) They can be exploited to create denial-of-service attacks

D. They always need a router to function

279. What is Tripwire in the context of Host-Based Intrusion Detection Systems (HIDS)?

A) A firewall program

B) A network monitoring tool

C) A file integrity monitoring program

D) An access control list manager

280. What is the main disadvantage of a manual response to IDS alerts?

A) It is too expensive

B) It is prone to operator inattention

C) It cannot be integrated with other systems

D) It takes too long to set up

281. Which of the following is considered the third generation of Intrusion Detection Systems (IDS)?

A) Intrusion Detection with automated response

B) Intrusion Detection with communication to firewalls and routers

C) Intrusion Prevention Systems (IPS)

D) Basic Intrusion Detection Systems without automated response

282. In cryptography, what does the 'A' in the CIA triad stand for?

A) Availability

B) Authenticity

C) Authorization

D) Auditability

283. What is the primary goal of cryptography?

A) Authenticity

B) Integrity

C) Secrecy

D) Nonrepudiation

284. What guarantees the message's authenticity and integrity in cryptography and ensures that it has not been modified?

A) Encryption

B) Nonrepudiation of origin

C) Key clustering

D) Cryptanalysis

285. What is key escrow primarily used for in cryptography?

A) To increase the complexity of the cryptosystem

B) To recover lost encryption keys

C) To create a backup of all cryptographic keys

D) To distribute keys to the user community

286. What does the work factor in cryptography refer to?

A) The cost of the cryptosystem

B) The amount of effort to maintain the cryptosystem

C) The time and resources required to defeat the cryptosystem

D) The duration for which the cryptosystem keeps the message secret

287. What is ciphertext in the context of cryptography?

A) The original message before encryption

B) The encrypted message that is unreadable without decryption

C) The algorithm used for transforming data

D) The key used to encrypt the message

288. According to Kerckhoff's Principle, what should be the only secret component of a cryptosystem?

A) The cryptographic algorithm

B) The encryption key

C) The plaintext message

D) The method of key distribution

289. What is the process of converting ciphertext back into plaintext called?

A) Enciphering

B) Key clustering

C) Deciphering

D) Cryptanalysis

290. What is the purpose of key clustering in cryptography?

A) To provide multiple keys for the same encrypted data

B) To store keys in a secure yet accessible manner

C) To allow another key to encrypt and decrypt data

D) To distribute keys to various individuals for emergency purposes

291. What is the primary challenge associated with private key cryptography?

A) Speed of encryption and decryption

B) Scalability to large numbers of users

C) Complexity of the encryption algorithm

D) Public availability of the encryption key

292. What is a significant security risk when distributing private keys?

A) The keys can be too complex for users to remember.

B) The keys may be sent over insecure channels like email or fax.

C) The encryption method may be very slow for practical use.

D) The keys are often very long to be transmitted efficiently.

293. What is a common problem with the strength of private keys?

A) They are very complex and cause the system to slow down.

B) They are often weak because humans create them.

C) They are difficult to change once set.

D) They are very lengthy to remember.

294. Which of the following is considered a legacy cryptosystem, having been largely supplanted by AES?

A) ECB

B) RSA

C) Triple-DES (3DES)

D) ECC

295. What is the main reason the U.S. government stopped supporting the clipper chip?

A) It was very slow.

B) It was not secure.

C) It failed to encrypt properly.

D) Public outcry forced the government to stop supporting it.

296. Which mode of DES operation functions as a stream cipher?

A) Electronic Code Book (ECB)

B) Cipher Block Chaining (CBC)

C) Cipher Feedback Mode (CFB)

D) Output Feedback Mode (OFB)

297. What is the mathematical foundation of public key cryptography?

A) Factoring very large prime numbers

B) Solving complex polynomial equations

C) Finding two points on a parabola

D) Generating random key streams

298. What is the major advantage of public key cryptography over private key cryptography?

A) It is faster.

B) It allows for better scalability.

C) It requires fewer resources.

D) It is simpler to understand.

299. What is the purpose of the certificate revocation list in public key cryptography?

A) To list weak keys in the server that issued them

B) To keep track of all the issued keys

C) To enhance the encryption process

D) To store backup copies of keys

300. Which algorithm was selected for the Advanced Encryption Standard (AES)?

A) DES

B) Skipjack

C) Rijndael

D) RSA

301. What is the primary purpose of using a stream cipher in cryptography?

A) To decrypt a message

B) To encrypt the message a bit at a time

C) To create a digital signature

D) To generate a hash function

302. Which of the following is NOT a rule that must apply to a key stream generator?

A) The key stream must be statistically unpredictable.

B) The key stream must repeat after short periods.

C) The key stream must be functionally complex.

D) The key stream cannot be easily related to the key.

303. What encryption protocol used by wireless networks employs a stream cipher?

A) SSL

B) AES

C) WEP

D) RSA

304. What is an Initialization Vector (IV) primarily used for in cryptography?

A) To generate a public key

B) To make encrypted messages appear different

C) To create a hash function

D) To decrypt a message

305. Which cryptographic concept involves using part of the previous message's ciphertext to create a more random-appearing key?

A) One-time pad

B) Hashing

C) Initialization Vector

D) Cipher Block Chaining (CBC)

306. What is the most common type of cryptanalysis attack mentioned in the text?

A) Timing attack

B) Chosen plaintext attack

C) Ciphertext-only attack

D) Rubber hose cryptanalysis

307. Which of the following is NOT a method used in cryptanalysis?

A) Brute force attack

B) Man-in-the-middle attack

C) Known plaintext attack

D) Symmetric encryption

308. What is the main goal of a digital signature in cryptography?

A) To encrypt a message

B) To hash a message

C) To ensure the integrity and authenticate the sender of a message

D) To create a key stream

309. Which algorithm is mentioned as generating a 128-bit electronic fingerprint?

A) SHA

B) RC4

C) DES

D) MD5

310. What is the primary function of hash functions like MD5 and SHA in cryptography?

A) To encrypt messages

B) To verify the integrity of information

C) To generate private keys

D) To create digital certificates

311. What type of cipher involves replacing one letter from the plaintext message with another character to encrypt the message?

A) Transposition Cipher

B) Poly-Alphabetic Cipher

C) Running Key Cipher

D) Substitution Cipher

312. How does a Caesar cipher encrypt a message?

A) By reversing the sequence of the letters

B) By replacing each letter with a number

C) By shifting the alphabet by a set number of spaces

D) By hiding the message in a picture or music file

313. What is the main difference between a substitution cipher and a transposition cipher?

A) Substitution ciphers use images; transposition ciphers do not.

B) Substitution ciphers change the alphabet used; transposition ciphers change the order of letters.

C) Substitution ciphers replace numbers with letters; transposition ciphers do not.

D) Substitution ciphers encrypt numbers; transposition ciphers encrypt letters.

314. What is a poly-alphabetic cipher?

A) A cipher that uses multiple alphabets to encrypt a message

B) A cipher that changes the positions of letters within the same alphabet

C) A cipher that uses pictures to hide messages

D) A cipher that encrypts messages using a key of pre-agreed upon characters

315. How does a running key cipher work?

A) By hiding a message in plain sight in a picture or music file

B) By using a pre-agreed upon set of characters to convey messages

C) By reversing the order of letters in a message

D) By using a secret decoder ring

316. What is the principle behind steganography?

A) Switching the least-significant bits of a file to hide a message

B) Using a secret decoder ring

C) Encrypting messages with a machine

D) Skipping words to hide a message

317. What is the difference between steganography and cryptography?

A) Cryptography hides messages in plain sight; steganography does not.

B) Steganography hides messages in plain sight, cryptography does not.

C) Steganography uses physical objects to hide messages, cryptography uses digital means.

D) Cryptography is always used by terrorist organizations, steganography is not.

318. What is an example of a code used to hide messages?

A) Caesar Cipher

B) Pig Latin

C) Enigma Machine

D) Transposition Cipher

319. What was the Enigma machine?

A) A steganography tool

B) A transposition cipher device

C) An encryption machine used in World War II

D) A type of running key cipher

320. Which cipher involves writing all the letters of a word in reverse order?

A) Substitution Cipher

B) Poly-Alphabetic Cipher

C) Running Key Cipher

D) Transposition Cipher

321. What is the primary purpose of the initial key exchange in an SSL session?

A) To encrypt the session key using symmetric encryption

B) To transmit the server's digital certificate to the client

C) To exchange a session key using public key encryption

D) To authenticate the client to the server using a digital signature

322. Which of the following is NOT a component of a cipher suite used in SSL?

A) Session key

B) Encryption algorithm

C) Hash function

D) Protocol version

323. In the context of SSL, what does a Certificate Authority (CA) do?

A) Encrypts data with the server's public key

B) Generates session keys for symmetric encryption

C) Signs digital certificates used in the SSL handshake

D) Manages the distribution of private keys to clients

324. What does the client check after receiving the server's digital certificate in SSL?

A) The certificate's encryption strength

B) Whether the certificate is on the client's trusted list of CAs

C) The private key contained within the certificate

D) The validity of the session key

325. What is the role of a Message Authentication Code (MAC) in securing communications?

A) To encrypt messages using public key cryptography

B) To verify the integrity and authenticity of a message using symmetric cryptography

C) To establish a secure SSL session between a client and a server

D) To distribute public keys in a Public Key Infrastructure (PKI)

326. What is the primary function of an IPSEC Encapsulated Secure Payload (ESP)?

A) To replace the original IP header for routing purposes

B) To encrypt the data portion of packets in transit

C) To authenticate one IPSEC device to another

D) To manage the certificate revocation list (CRL)

327. What does a risk table help an information security manager determine?

A) The encryption algorithms to use in a cipher suite

B) The likelihood and impact of risks to the organization

C) The correct wireless standard to implement

D) The appropriate baseline controls for a system

328. What is a baseline in the context of information security controls?

A) A cryptographic algorithm used in SSL sessions

B) A minimum set of controls for systems with low sensitivity levels

C) A list of wireless standards

D) A protocol used for secure IP communications

329. Which of the following is true about Certificate Authorities (CAs) within PKI?

A) They are always separate from the registration authority

B) They directly manage the Certificate Revocation List (CRL)

C) They publish public keys for users to verify private keys

D) They encrypt data with the server's public key

330. What is the primary security function of the IPSEC Authentication Header (AH)?

A) To encrypt IP data payloads

B) To replace the original IP header for authentication purposes

C) To authenticate IP packets and ensure their integrity

D) To manage the distribution of symmetric keys

331. What frequency band does the 802.11b wireless standard operate on?

A) 5 GHz

B) 2.4 GHz

C) 49 MHz

D) 900 MHz

332. What is the maximum data rate that 802.11g wireless networks can handle?

A) 11 megabits per second

B) 28 megabits per second

C) 54 megabits per second

D) 100 megabits per second

333. Which wireless encryption standard was the first used to protect confidentiality?

A) WPA

B) WEP

C) 802.1x

D) AES

334. What does WEP stand for?

A) Wireless Encryption Protocol

B) Wired Equivalent Privacy

C) Wireless Encryption Privacy

D) Wired Encryption Protocol

335. How many bits are in the older WEP encryption variation?

A) 64-bit

B) 40-bit

C) 128-bit

D) 104-bit

336. Which statement is true regarding the backward compatibility of 802.11g networks?

A) They are not backward compatible with any other standard.

B) They are backward compatible with 802.11a networks.

C) They are backward compatible with 802.11b networks.

D) They are backward compatible with 802.11n networks.

337. Which technique does 802.11b use for encoding?

A) OFDM

B) CCK

C) WPA2

D) AES

338. What does the Initialization Vector (IV) do in WEP encryption?

A) It encrypts the key itself.

B) It is used to verify the integrity of the message.

C) It provides a starting point for the pseudo-random number generator.

D) It is sent encrypted with each packet.

339. What is the major vulnerability of the WEP's Integrity Check Value (ICV)?

A) It can be decrypted with a simple algorithm.

B) It uses a linear function that allows packet modification.

C) It is only 24 bits long.

D) It uses a complex hash function.

340. What is the primary weakness of WEP encryption that attackers exploit, regardless of key size?

A) The encryption algorithm itself is weak.

B) The encryption keys are too long.

C) IV and ICV-based attacks.

D) The encryption keys are too short.

341. What is the main purpose of using WEP on a wireless network?

A) To authenticate users accessing the network

B) To increase the network's bandwidth

C) To encrypt the data transmitted over the network

D) To assign IP addresses to the wireless clients

342. What is a major problem with the existing 802.11 standard regarding WEP keys?

A) WEP keys do not provide encryption.

B) WEP keys are easy to decrypt even without tools.

C) WEP keys are cumbersome to change and update often.

D) WEP keys automatically change every five minutes.

343. What does 802.1x use to provide an effective framework for authenticating and controlling user traffic to a protected network?

A) WEP

B) EAP (Extensible Authentication Protocol)

C) PPP (Point to Point Protocol)

D) RADIUS

344. Which EAP method is considered the only standard secure option for wireless LANs at the time of the given text?

A) EAP-MD5

B) Cisco's LEAP

C) EAP-TLS

D) EAP-TTLS

345. What is the role of RADIUS in an 802.1x setup?

A) It encrypts data packets.

B) It authenticates user identity.

C) It changes WEP keys automatically.

D) It distributes IP addresses.

346. What term does 802.1x use to refer to the client attempting to connect to the network?

A) Authenticator

B) Authentication server

C) Supplicant

D) Access point

347. What type of attack does mutual authentication in Cisco's LEAP method help to reduce?

A) Denial-of-Service (DoS) attack

B) Man-in-the-Middle (MitM) attack

C) Phishing attack

D) SQL Injection attack

348. In the context of 802.1x, what is an 'authenticator'?

A) The client device

B) The WAP (Wireless Access Point)

C) The encryption protocol

D) The RADIUS server

349. How often can encryption keys be changed in typical 802.1x implementations to prevent eavesdroppers from cracking the current key?

A) Every hour

B) As often as necessary, with a common default of every five minutes

C) Once a day

D) Every time a user logs in

350. Which of the following is not a function of 802.1x?

A) Providing a framework for user authentication

B) Dynamically varying encryption keys

C) Acting as an authentication mechanism

D) Controlling user traffic to a protected network

351. What was the primary reason for the development of TKIP?

A) To provide backward compatibility with older hardware.

B) To allow easy firmware updates.

C) To correct the weak WEP problem.

D) To replace the CRC-32 integrity check.

352. Which encryption algorithm does TKIP use?

A) AES

B) RC4

C) CRC-32

D) MIC

353. What is the function of the Message Integrity Check (MIC) in TKIP?

A) To encrypt the data payload.

B) To verify the integrity of the data and prevent packet modification.

C) To hash the initialization vector values.

D) To generate a new encryption key.

354. Which standard includes TKIP among its security features?

A) 802.1x

B) WPA

C) WEP

D) AES

355. What does WPA-PSK stand for?

A) Wi-Fi Protected Access - Public Shared Key

B) Wi-Fi Protected Access - Personal Secure Key

C) Wi-Fi Protected Access - Pre-Shared Key

D) Wi-Fi Protected Access - Private Security Key

356. What major security risk does WPA2 address by incorporating the new AES algorithm?

A) Incompatibility with older hardware.

B) The single level of WE-based open authentication.

C) The ease of sniffing IVs out of the air.

D) Buffer overflow vulnerabilities.

357. When did 802.11i become a full standard?

A) July 29, 2004

B) November 10, 2006

C) January 1, 2005

D) December 31, 2003

358. What is a buffer overflow?

A) A method of encryption.

B) An error in programming that can lead to security breaches.

C) A type of VPN connection.

D) A protocol for wireless security.

359. What type of VPN is typically used by teleworkers to access the corporate network?

A) Site-to-Site VPN

B) Client-to-Site VPN

C) IPSEC VPN

D) SSL VPN

360. Which mechanism is typically responsible for Internet security, distinguishing between legitimate web traffic and potential attacks?

A) Web Server

B) VPN

C) Firewall with deep packet inspection or intrusion prevention

D) TKIP

361. What is the primary goal of a penetration test?

A) To assess policy and procedure compliance

B) To break into the system

C) To identify technical and non-technical vulnerabilities

D) To evaluate the impact on the organization

362. What is a vulnerability assessment typically used to identify?

A) The toughness of white-hat hackers

B) The structure and repeatability of security measures

C) Gaps in the security controls of a system

D) How an organization's reputation can be affected by a breach

363. What is a characteristic feature of a risk assessment in security testing?

A) It is technically focused

B) It involves breaking into the system

C) It is concerned with the impact on the organization

D) It is conducted by white-hat hackers

364. Which of the following is NOT a typical element of a penetration test?

A) Social engineering

B) Checking for policy compliance

C) Employing white-hat hackers

D) Aiming to breach system defenses

365. How does a vulnerability assessment differ from a penetration test?

A) It is less structured

B) It is more focused on breaking in

C) It is more comprehensive and can include policy issues

D) It is conducted post-breach

366. Which type of security testing would involve trying to break in through people?

A) Vulnerability assessment

B) Penetration testing

C) Risk assessment

D) Firewall inspection

367. What does a hybrid approach to security testing involve?

A) Combining risk assessment with firewall inspection

B) Using only white-hat hackers in testing

C) Bundling different approaches, such as vulnerability and penetration testing

D) Focusing solely on technical school methodologies

368. At what stage of the security life cycle is a vulnerability assessment typically conducted?

A) As the first element

B) Midway through the cycle

C) One of the last elements

D) Immediately after a breach

369. What is the focus of a penetration test compared to a vulnerability assessment?

A) Broad and comprehensively focused

B) Non-technical and focused on impact

C) Narrow and technically focused

D) Structured and repeatable focus

370. Which security test is described as 'very narrowly focused' and akin to going to technical school?

A) Risk assessment

B) Vulnerability assessment

C) Penetration testing

D) Firewall inspection

371. What is the primary difference between a pure peer-to-peer network and a hybrid peer-to-peer network?

A) Pure peer-to-peer networks have a central server that keeps information on peers.

B) Hybrid peer-to-peer networks have no central server managing the network.

C) Pure peer-to-peer networks identify equal peer nodes that simultaneously function as both clients and servers.

D) Hybrid peer-to-peer networks do not use a central router.

372. What is NOT one of the responsibilities outlined in administrative procedures for information systems compliance?

A) Media handling

B) System and equipment maintenance

C) Designing the graphical user interface of the system

D) Contingency plans

373. Who should be responsible for writing procedures according to the text?

A) A management team

B) Subject Matter Experts (SMEs) solely

C) A technical writer with input from SMEs

D) External consultants

374. What is the purpose of a change management process in information systems?

A) To upgrade systems without authorization

B) To control and approve modifications to the IT infrastructure

C) To eliminate the need for backup or disaster recovery plans

D) To increase the complexity of the IT environment

375. Which of the following is NOT one of the requirements for procedure writing?

A) Keeping sentences short and simple

B) Using a passive voice to describe actions

C) Ensuring grammar and punctuation are correct

D) Using clear, familiar words

376. During the change management process, who should NOT test the procedure?

A) The technical writer

B) The subject matter expert

C) An individual unfamiliar with the subject

D) A person filling in for the SME

377. What should the procurement and contracts policy include regarding third-party security controls?

A) A confidentiality or nondisclosure agreement

B) A clause allowing third parties to define security measures

C) Permission for third parties to bypass security audits

D) Freedom for third parties to change security policies without approval

378. What is a critical control element in the separation of duties related to change control?

A) Combining responsibility for program changes with updating the production environment

B) Separating responsibility for program changes from testing and updating the production environment

C) Allowing developers to perform all changes without oversight

D) Eliminating the need for a rollback or disaster recovery plan

379. What should be included in the service delivery contract when outsourcing?

A) Only the financial aspects of the service

B) Agreed-upon security arrangements and service definitions

C) An agreement to avoid service management

D) A clause that exempts the third party from adhering to service-level agreements

380. Why is it important for the contracting organization to be a member of the third-party's change management process?

A. To make changes to the provision of the service level agreements

B. To take responsibility for the third party's security policies

C. To control the third party's internal management

D. To avoid any involvement in the third party's operational processes

381. What is the primary role of Senior Management in measuring the effectiveness of an Information Security (IS) program?

A) Implement a program to measure IS effectiveness

B) Approve policies, standards, and procedures

C) Provide sufficient resources to complete the assessment

D) Report to Senior Management of the state of the IS program

382. Which of the following is NOT a component of an effective security program?

A) Practical security policies and procedures

B) Developing and establishing quantifiable performance metrics

C) Consistent periodic analysis of performance data

D) Elimination of all security risks

383. What is the purpose of Key Performance Indicators (KPIs) in an information security program?

A) To ensure that all vulnerabilities are patched

B) To help the organization define and measure progress toward goals

C) To focus solely on technical aspects of security

D) To approve the budget for security expenditures

384. What is the role of the security administrator during the change management process?

A) To approve all change requests

B) To analyze and assess the impact of all changes to the production environment

C) To provide financial resources for change implementation

D) To eliminate the need for change control

385. What is Risk Transference in the context of risk mitigation?

A) Accepting the potential risk and continuing operations

B) Eliminating the risk cause or consequences

C) Transferring the risk using other options to compensate for the loss

D) Limiting the risk by implementing controls

386. What is the purpose of performing Vulnerability Assessments?

A) To sell security products to the organization

B) To evaluate the effectiveness of existing controls

C) To train security personnel

D) To implement new security policies

387. What factors may limit the depth of a Network Vulnerability Assessment (NVA)?

A) The complexity of the organization's website

B) The time and cost associated with conducting the NVA

C) The number of employees in the organization

D) The geographic location of the organization

388. What should a technical network vulnerability assessment report typically include?

A) Only a summary for senior management

B) A detailed technical manual for IT staff only

C) Specific vulnerability findings and a summary of various audience segments

D) A financial statement for the accounting department

389. What type of vulnerabilities are often referred to as "bugs" that can be fixed with service packs and hotfixes?

A) Soft vulnerabilities

B) Hard vulnerabilities

C) Phreaker vulnerabilities

D) Hacker vulnerabilities

390. What is the difference between a hacker and a cracker?

A) A hacker is an enthusiast, while a cracker breaks into systems maliciously

B) A cracker is a professional programmer, while a hacker lacks formal training

C) A hacker and a cracker are the same

D) A cracker is a slang term for a computer enthusiast

391. What is the primary role of a CISO in the context of compliance and intellectual property rights?

A) To conduct regular reviews of employee compliance levels.

B) To implement specific controls and identify individual responsibilities.

C) To provide legal counsel on monitoring procedures.

D) To design the information security awareness and education program.

392. What should be included at log-on to indicate monitoring of user activities?

A) A welcome message to the user.

B) A list of all users currently logged in.

C) A warning message indicating authorized use and monitoring.

D) A disclaimer of liability for the organization.

393. What is a key component of ensuring that information reflects the real status of an organization?

A) Regular software updates.

B) Effective change management.

C) Confidentiality of information.

D) A robust marketing strategy.

394. Which of the following best describes the concept of 'Due Care'?

A) The obligation to act in the best interest of another party.

B) The care a reasonable person would exercise under the circumstances.

C) A measure of prudence and assessment by a reasonable person.

D) The obligation to act in the best interest of the organization.

395. What is the purpose of compliance terms in the context of information security management?

A) To define technical specifications for software development.

B) To outline the legal responsibilities and rights of employees.

C) To establish guidelines for the company's marketing strategies.

D) To provide instructions for hardware maintenance.

396. Which of the following is NOT an element of the information security program presented to the audience?

A) Steps to reinforce that security is part of the business process.

B) Identification of responsible individuals for security implementation.

C) The sensitivity of information and criticality of applications.

D) Annual financial reports of the organization.

397. What is the primary objective of an information security awareness program?

A) To increase the technical skills of the IT staff.

B) To make employees aware of their rights and responsibilities.

C) To sell security software to other companies.

D) To conduct vulnerability assessments.

398. What is the function of technical compliance checking?

A) To evaluate the physical security of the premises.

B) To assess the organization's financial health.

C) To examine operational systems for correct control implementation.

D) To oversee the company's recruitment process.

399. Which compliance term defines the obligation of an individual to act in the best interest of the organization?

A) Fiduciary Duty

B) Duty of Loyalty

C) Duty of Fairness

D) Corporate Opportunity

400. Which term refers to a person's right to prevent others from copying works they have created, which lasts for the author's lifetime plus 95 years?

A) Trademark

B) Patent

C) Copyright

D) Trade Secret

401. What is the primary goal of an ongoing information security awareness program?

A) To discipline employees who breach security protocols

B) To inform employees about what is expected of them and where to seek help

C) To monitor employee activities constantly

D) To enforce strict security measures without explanation

402. How often should mandatory refresher classes and sessions for information security be held, according to the text?

A) Weekly

B) Monthly

C) Quarterly

D) At least annually

403. Who should ideally conduct awareness training for contract personnel?

A) The organization's senior management

B) The contract house employing the personnel

C) Regular employees

D) Third-party security consultants

404. What was the Quality of Work Life (QWL) concept introduced in the 1970s aimed at addressing?

A) The efficiency of the production line

B) Employee feelings about their job, bosses, and fellow employees

C) The implementation of information technology

D) The financial benefits for employees

405. What is the "Ladder of Inference" associated with?

A) Total Quality Management (TQM)

B) Quality of Work Life (QWL)

C) Learning Organization

D) Information Security Management

406. When should special dates be incorporated into an information security program's calendar of events?

A) Only during security breaches

B) When the CEO is present

C) On dates like International Emergency Response Day and International Computer Security Day

D) At random to maintain unpredictability

407. What should the message of the information security program ideally show to the employees?

A) The complexity of security measures

B) The benefits and importance of security measures to them

C) The consequences of not following security protocols

D) The technical details of the security infrastructure

408. What is one suggested way to assess the current level of sophistication in computer usage among employees?

A) Implementing advanced security software

B) Asking questions and being an effective listener

C) Assigning computer-based tests

D) Reviewing the IT department's reports

409. How can you identify which managers support the objectives of the security program?

A) By observing their behavior in meetings

B) By assessing their department's financial performance

C) By seeking out managers who have the respect of their peers

D) By checking the number of security incidents in their departments

410. What approach is recommended when introducing new controls or policies to management?

A) Implementing them immediately without discussion

B) Discussing and reviewing the changes individually with managers

C) Sending a detailed email to all managers

D) Presenting the changes in a large, company-wide meeting

411. What is the recommended maximum duration for a standard awareness presentation?

A) 20 minutes

B) 30 minutes

C) 45 minutes

D) 50 minutes

412. What should be prepared for a meeting with business unit managers?

A) A 10-minute presentation with a one-page summary

B) A 20-minute individual meeting with two or three pages of materials

C) A 45-minute presentation with a full report

D) A 30-minute group session with visual aids

413. What is the suggested length of time for senior management's awareness presentation?

A) 15 minutes

B) 30 minutes

C) 45 minutes

D) 60 minutes

414. What is the KISS practice in the context of information security awareness programs?

A) Keeping Information Security Simple

B) Keep It Short and Simple

C) Keep It Simple, Sweetie

D) Know It, Share It, Secure It

415. What is a key consideration when conveying a message to an audience according to Neural-linguistic programming?

A) Age of the audience

B) Professional background of the presenter

C) Learning styles of the audience

D) The presenter's personal experiences

416. What is the primary way people obtain news and information that should be considered when designing an awareness program?

A) Books

B) Television or radio

C) Newspapers

D) Internet

417. What is the role of the information security coordinators in decentralized organizations?

A) To manage senior executive schedules

B) To conduct risk assessments for the information security infrastructure

C) To present the awareness sessions to their specific organization

D) To provide technical support for the information security group

418. What is an effective way to reinforce the security message post-presentation?

A) Scheduling follow-up meetings

B) Handing out disciplinary notices for non-compliance

C) Providing booklets, brochures, or promotional items

D) Implementing a strict dress code

419. How should you prepare for effective communication during an awareness program?

A) Dress in a way that is less formal than the audience

B) Speak using a lot of technical jargon for credibility

C) Prepare and test all materials and audio-visuals beforehand

D) Plan for a two-hour long presentation to cover all topics

420. What is a useful ice-breaker, as suggested in the text?

A) A role-playing game

B) A personality test using word association

C) A technical quiz

D) A group discussion on security breaches

421. When is the best time to schedule an awareness session?

A) Monday morning

B) After lunch

C) Friday afternoon

D) Tuesday morning

422. What is the "stunned owl" syndrome?

A) When people are extremely focused during presentations

B) When words seem to hit the audience in the forehead and fall to the floor

C) When people are excited about the content of the session

D) When the audience asks many questions during a presentation

423. What should be avoided when scheduling an awareness session?

A) Morning sessions

B) Sessions after lunch

C) Brief presentations

D) Off-shift hours

424. What type of presentation is preferred by senior management?

A) Long and detailed with videos

B) Brief and concise with in-depth supporting documentation

C) Interactive with a personality test

D) Slides and a detailed agenda

425. What should you not do when presenting to senior management?

A) Present a problem without a solution

B) Discuss the issues

C) Provide supporting documentation

D) Explain the purpose of the program

426. How can managers be won over to new security controls?

A) By showing how they will slow down processes

B) By demonstrating improved performance processes

C) By having a lengthy discussion on security

D) By reducing their level of responsibility

427. What is the general attitude of line supervisors and employees towards company initiatives?

A) Enthusiastic and supportive

B) Skeptical and passive

C) Indifferent and unresponsive

D) Excited and proactive

428. What role do employees play in the protection of information assets?

A) They have no responsibility

B) They are solely responsible for its protection

C) They must ensure it supports management-approved activities

D) They should report any misuse to senior management

429. What is the scope of an effective information security program?

A) Limited to computer-held data

B) Covering all information, wherever it is found

C) Focused on senior management's activities

D) Only for new employees

430. What is a key focus when updating an existing out-dated information security program?

A) Convincing employees that no changes are needed

B) Convincing management of the need for change

C) Disregarding industry benchmarks

D) Reducing the overall cost of the program

431. What is the definition of a disaster according to the Disaster Recovery Journal?

A) A minor disruption in service that causes inconvenience.

B) A planned event that brings about significant improvements.

C) A sudden, unplanned, calamitous event causing great damage or loss.

D) A routine maintenance activity that temporarily halts business operations.

432. What is considered an incident by the Disaster Recovery Journal?

A) An event causing a service disruption lasting less than 24 hours.

B) A catastrophic event leading to permanent damage to the organization.

C) A pre-planned exercise to test organizational resilience.

D) Any security breach, regardless of its impact or duration.

433. Which of the following is a source for understanding the latest threats to information security systems?

A) Internet Service Providers

B) Security research organizations

C) Marketing analysis firms

D) International trade bodies

434. What should be the first step in prioritizing threats to an organization?

A) Estimating the financial impact of each threat.

B) Determining the likelihood and frequency of each threat.

C) Creating a disaster recovery plan for each potential threat.

D) Purchasing insurance for the most expensive threats.

435. What is a critical function that an Intrusion Detection System (IDS) should have?

A) The ability to function as a firewall.

B) The capability to modify and adapt to new exploits.

C) A feature to automatically patch software vulnerabilities.

D) The power to enforce company policy on acceptable use.

436. What should an IDS be able to detect in an organization's environment?

A) Employee productivity levels.

B) Anomalies from the baseline of normal processing.

C) The financial impact of an attack.

D) The content of encrypted network traffic.

437. What is an important aspect of an IDS system's audit logs?

A) They can predict future attacks.

B) They can be backed up or spooled off to another device.

C) They are accessible to all employees for transparency.

D) They encrypt all log entries for confidentiality.

438. What is the role of the Information Security Manager when a control fails or a new threat emerges?

A) To eliminate the threat immediately without analysis.

B) To take a leave until the threat is neutralized by technical staff.

C) To manage the incident or disaster resulting from the failure.

D) To outsource the problem to a third-party vendor.

439. Which statement best describes the relationship between the number of threats and information security budgets?

A) The number of threats decreases as information security budgets increase.

B) Information security budgets are always sufficient to cover all threats.

C) The number of threats increases every year, but budgets do not necessarily increase.

D) Budgets are prioritized based on the number of successful attacks in the past year.

440. What is the main goal of a Business Continuity Plan (BCP)?

A) To recover the IT infrastructure after a disaster

B) To ensure continuous IT support only

C) To assist the organization in continuing functions during disruptions

D) To replace the need for insurance in a disaster

441. What is the Disaster Recovery Plan (DRP) primarily responsible for?

A) Managing the entire business operations during a disaster

B) Planning for non-IT related contingencies

C) Recovery of the information technology infrastructure

D) Handling media communications during a disaster

442. How often should a Business Continuity Plan be tested according to best practices?

A) Biannually

B) Quarterly

C) At least annually

D) Every month

443. Who is responsible for creating a policy regarding BCP?

A) Functional managers

B) Auditors

C) Executive (senior) management

D) IT department

444. What is the Business Recovery Plan (BRP) primarily concerned with?

A) Sustaining business functions during a disruption

B) Restoring business processes after an emergency

C) Ensuring the continuity of IT operations

D) Planning for long-term recovery and return to normal operations

445. What is NOT a reason for Business Continuity Planning to fail within an organization?

A) Lack of senior management support

B) High costs of development

C) Too frequent testing of the plan

D) Done in response to an outside force

446. What is the Continuity of Operations Plan (COOP) focused on?

A) Restoring IT operations at an alternate site

B) Restoring headquarters-level functions at an alternate site

C) Ensuring continuity of critical processes during an emergency

D) Providing support for minor disruptions that do not require relocation

447. What should the Continuity of Support Plan contain?

A) Only the recovery strategies for business processes

B) The development and maintenance of continuity of support plans for systems and applications

C) A plan for how to communicate with the media during a disaster

D) The identification of all possible natural disasters

448. Which plan is not necessarily included in a Business Continuity Plan (BCP)?

A) Business Recovery Plan (BRP)

B) Disaster Recovery Plan (DRP)

C) Cyber Incident Response Plan

D) Continuity of Operations Plan (COOP)

449. What is a secondary benefit of the BCP process?

A) It replaces the need for insurance

B) It identifies critical resources, assets, and dependent systems

C) It ensures the IT department is the main focus during a disaster

D) It provides a clear chain of command during non-disaster times

450. What is the primary purpose of a Crisis Communications Plan within an organization?

A) To coordinate social media marketing campaigns.

B) To establish procedures to address cyber attacks.

C) To prepare internal and external communications procedures prior to a disaster.

D) To provide response procedures for fire drills and medical emergencies.

451. What is the main focus of a Cyber Incident Response Plan?

A) To provide a response for physical security breaches.

B) To establish procedures to address cyber attacks against an organization's IT systems.

C) To restore all systems simultaneously after a disaster.

D) To handle media inquiries during a crisis.

452. What does DRP stand for, and when is it typically invoked?

A) Disaster Recovery Plan; during minor disruptions.

B) Data Retrieval Plan; during routine system maintenance.

C) Disaster Response Protocol; when access to the normal facility is denied for an extended period.

D) Disaster Recovery Plan; when access to the normal facility is denied for an extended period.

453. What is an Occupant Emergency Plan (OEP) designed to address?

A) Cybersecurity threats and data breaches.

B) Situations posing a potential threat to the health and safety of building occupants.

C) The order in which business systems should be restored after an incident.

D) Communication strategies for dealing with the media during a crisis.

454. In the context of Business Continuity Planning (BCP), what does BIA stand for, and what is its purpose?

A) Business Impact Analysis, to bring up all systems simultaneously after a disaster.

B) Business Integration Assessment, to merge IT systems with business processes.

C) Business Impact Analysis, to determine which systems are critical and should be restored first.

D) Business Infrastructure Audit, to assess the physical condition of the company's facilities.

455. Which of the following can complicate performing a Business Impact Analysis (BIA)?

A) The simplicity of systems.

B) Lack of office politics.

C) System dependencies and complexity.

D) Having too few systems to analyze.

456. What is the Maximum Tolerable Outage (MTO) as used in a BIA?

A) The minimum amount of time to complete an inventory of IT systems.

B) The duration of a typical system backup process.

C) The maximum amount of time that a system can be offline before the business cannot recover.

D) The timeframe in which a cyber incident must be reported to authorities.

457. What is the typical outcome of a Business Impact Analysis (BIA)?

A) A detailed budget for the IT department.

B) A list of employees to be contacted during a disaster.

C) The overall criticality of systems and Recovery Time Objectives (RTOs).

D) The blueprint for the company's IT network infrastructure.

458. Why might office politics play a role in the outcome of a BIA?

A) Because employees may feel their job security is threatened if their systems are not rated highest in criticality.

B) Because it determines who gets promoted within the company.

C) Because it influences the company's stock price.

D) Because it dictates the annual budget allocation for departments.

459. What is one of the goals of performing a Business Impact Analysis (BIA)?

A) To reduce the amount of time spent on IT audits.

B) To understand operational impacts and determine recovery timeframes.

C) To select the best software for inventory management.

D) To establish a new marketing strategy for the organization.

460. What is the primary purpose of a Business Impact Analysis (BIA)?

A) To determine the budget for the information security department

B) To select the appropriate alternate site for system requirements

C) To identify critical business processes and maximum tolerable downtime

D) To train new employees on business continuity procedures

461. Which of the following is NOT a type of alternate site mentioned in NIST 800-34?

A) Warm Sites

B) Cool Sites

C) Cold Sites

D) Mobile Sites

462. Which type of alternate site is fully equipped and typically staffed 24/7?

A) Cold Site

B) Warm Site

C) Hot Site

D) Mobile Site

463. What is the major drawback of Reciprocal Agreements, according to the text?

A) They are the most expensive option available.

B) They require long setup times.

C) They often fail due to the disruptive nature of co-locating processing.

D) They lack the necessary telecommunications infrastructure.

464. Which alternate site option has the highest degree of availability?

A) Cold Site

B) Warm Site

C) Mobile Site

D)Mirrored Site

465. When writing a Business Continuity Plan (BCP), what should be included?

A) Only the recovery strategies for IT equipment

B) Information on team training exclusively

C) Equipment location, purchase details, vendor contacts, and SLAs

D) Just the data backup strategy

466. Why is cross-training important in the context of a BCP?

A) To ensure employees are capable of handling multiple roles during a disaster

B) For the purpose of performance evaluation

C) To reduce the overall cost of training

D) To comply with international standards

467. What should the initial test of a BCP plan identify?

A) The most knowledgeable Subject Matter Expert (SME)

B) Missing steps due to the in-depth knowledge of the process

C) The budget needed for future plan improvements

D) The effectiveness of the company's marketing strategy

468. What should NOT occur during the testing of a BCP?

A) Involvement of all team members

B) Disruption of essential work or business processes

C) Appointment of a referee to ensure no cheating

D) Use of a detailed or high-level mock disaster scenario

469. What is a critical action to take after identifying areas for improvement in a BCP test?

A) Assigning tasks to responsible individuals

B) Increasing the budget for the BCP

C) Firing the Subject Matter Expert (SME)

D) Halting all business processes until improvements are made

470. What are the three phases of Business Continuity Planning (BCP) in disaster response?

A) Preparation, Response, Mitigation

B) Response, Recovery, Restoration

C) Identification, Response, Recovery

D) Prevention, Mitigation, Response

471. Who typically makes up the Crisis Management Team (CMT)?

A) IT staff, legal team, and operations management

B) Senior executives, PR staff, and HR staff

C) Security personnel, server recovery team, and procurement team

D) Alternate site recovery coordination team, test team, and administrative support team

472. When does an incident become a disaster in BCP?

A) After the response phase is complete

B) Once the Crisis Management Team has declared it

C) When the recovery strategy is implemented

D) As soon as the incident happens

473. What is the primary objective during the response phase of BCP?

A) To conduct surveillance

B) To conduct a business impact analysis

C) To stabilize the environment and protect people

D) To restore processing to Tier 1 and Tier 2 applications

474. Which team is responsible for heading out to the storage facility to locate tape backups of data?

A) The offsite storage team

B) The media relations team

C) The database recovery team

D) The hardware salvage team

475. What is the role of the salvage team in BCP?

A) To restore Tier 3 to 5 applications

B) To assess the initial damage and declare a disaster

C) To salvage whatever equipment is salvageable from the disaster site

D) To coordinate the recovery at an alternate site

476. What does the restoration team begin with during the resumption phase of BCP?

A) Bringing up Tier 1 and Tier 2 applications

B) Salvaging equipment

C) Bringing up Tier 3 to 5 applications

D) Parallel processing

477. What is the difference between an incident and a disaster, according to BCP?

A) An incident is less severe and typically creates an outage of 24 hours or less, whereas a disaster is more severe.

B) An incident and a disaster are the same; the terms can be used interchangeably.

C) An incident refers to unauthorized access, while a disaster refers to natural calamities.

D) A disaster requires a business impact analysis, while an incident does not.

478. Which document is one of the most commonly referenced for incident response?

A) Digital Investigative Framework

B) NIST Special Publication 800-34

C) NIST Special Publication 800-86

D) SB-1386

479. Who should be notified first upon the discovery of an event that could be a security incident?

A) The media

B) Law enforcement

C) Senior management

D) The public relations team

480. What is the primary goal of electronic surveillance?

A) To monitor social media activity

B) To detect changes in system or resource usage

C) To advertise products online

D) To provide entertainment to users

481. Which of the following is an example of a pay surveillance utility?

A) Beast

B) Guptachar

C) eBlaster

D) VNC

482. Who generally has more success in attacking systems, according to past trends?

A) Outsiders

B) Insiders

C) Hackers with advanced skills

D) Corporate spies

483. Which law enforcement agency is NOT mentioned as an option for investigating computer crimes?

A) State Police

B) CIA

C) FBI

D) County Police

484. What is the number one factor when running an investigation, according to the text?

A) Time

B) Privacy concerns

C) Cost

D) Availability of evidence

485. Which book is recommended for assistance with the interview and interrogation process?

A) Influence: Science and Practice

B) Essentials of the Reid Technique

C) The Art of Deception

D) The Principles of Kinesic Interview and Interrogation Technique

486. What should be done if all evidence points to an outsider during a computer crime investigation?

A) Hire a private investigator

B) Look for an insider colluding with the outsider

C) Immediately inform the media

D) Drop the investigation

487. Which principle of persuasion involves establishing credibility quickly with claims of authority?

A) Reciprocation

B) Social Validation

C) Scarcity

D) Authority

488. What percentage of reported laptop thefts can typically be recovered, according to the consulting company mentioned?

A) 30%

B) 50%

C) 70%

D) 90%

489. Who is generally responsible for coordinating all tasks during an investigation?

A) The head of IT

B) The lead investigator

C) The chief financial officer

D) The human resources representative

490. What is the first cardinal rule of system seizure in an investigation process?

A) Always use a digital camera

B) Do no harm

C) Pull the plug

D) Secure the suspect first

491. Which of the following is a common control used to secure the area during system seizure?

A) Hacking the system

B) Sign-in/sign-out sheet

C) Shutting down the system gracefully

D) Using a digital camera without a hash function

492. What should be captured to show the state of the system at the time of approach?

A) The contents of the CPU cache

B) The contents of the monitor

C) The serial number of the hard drive

D) The RAM data

493. What is a concern when using digital cameras for documenting evidence?

A) They are too expensive for practical use

B) Programs such as Photoshop can alter the media

C) Digital cameras cannot take pictures of screens

D) They create too large of a file size

494. What is live system forensics commonly used to investigate?

A) Hard drive defects

B) Inappropriate files

C) CPU performance

D) Network speed

495. When using the older forensic methodology, which is the most volatile source of information that should be gathered first?

A) RAM

B) CPU Cache

C) SWAP file

D) Network connection table

496. What is one disadvantage of using the older forensic methodology?

A) It's too time-consuming

B) It requires expert knowledge of Linux

C) The target system is modified during evidence collection

D) It cannot capture data from the hard drive

497. What is the main advantage of pulling the plug instead of shutting down the system gracefully?

A) It is faster and more convenient

B) It preserves the contents of the hard drive in the most pristine state

C) It ensures that all temporary files are saved

D) It allows the CPU cache to be dumped into a file

498. What is the main purpose of creating a bit-stream image during forensic processing?

A) To update the system's operating system

B) To backup only the files on the drive

C) To create a complete image of everything on a hard drive

D) To only capture files that have been recently accessed

499. What is the purpose of comparing MD5 hash values of the original and backup drives during forensic processing?

A) To ensure that the backup drive is larger

B) To confirm that the backup is an exact copy of the original

C) To check the speed of the backup process

D) To determine the brand of the hard drives

500. Which of the following best describes the role of the Information Security Steering Committee?

A) Implementing security controls

B) Assessing security risks

C) Providing strategic direction for information security

D) Monitoring compliance with security policies

501. What is the primary objective of an information security governance framework?

A) Ensuring regulatory compliance

B) Aligning information security with business objectives

C) Implementing technical security controls

D) Detecting and responding to security incidents

Information Risk Management:

502. Which of the following is a key component of the risk assessment process?

A) Identifying security incidents

B) Assessing the effectiveness of security controls

C) Implementing security policies

D) Monitoring network traffic

503. What is the purpose of a risk mitigation plan?

A) Eliminating all identified risks

B) Reducing the impact of identified risks to an acceptable level

C) Transferring all identified risks to a third party

D) Ignoring identified risks that fall below a certain threshold

Information Security Program Development and Management:

504. Which of the following is NOT typically included in an information security program?

A) Security awareness training for employees

B) Incident response procedures

C) Patch management for operating systems

D) Inventory management for physical assets

505. What is the primary responsibility of the Chief Information Security Officer (CISO) in managing an information security program?

A) Performing vulnerability assessments

B) Developing security policies

C) Ensuring alignment with business goals

D) Responding to security incidents

506. What is the purpose of an incident response plan?

A) Preventing security incidents from occurring

B) Identifying security incidents in real-time

C) Defining the steps to take in response to security incidents

D) Assigning blame for security incidents after they occur

507. During which phase of the incident management process are containment and eradication activities typically performed?

A) Detection

B) Analysis

C) Containment

D) Recovery

508. Which of the following best describes the concept of risk appetite?

A) The maximum amount of risk an organization is willing to accept

B) The likelihood of a security incident occurring

C) The effectiveness of security controls in mitigating risks

D) The financial impact of a security breach

Answers

1. **Answer:** C

Explanation: According to the governance roles and responsibilities, the Information Security Steering Committee's role is to establish and support the security program. This committee is typically chaired by the Chief Information Security Officer (CISO) and includes members such as the CEO, CFO, COO, and CTO, as well as the VP of Business Units.

2. **Answer:** C

Explanation: The three key elements necessary for successful security and privacy policies and procedures are that they must be documented, communicated, and current. While regular updates are important to maintain relevance.

3. **Answer:** B

Explanation: Two-factor authentication refers to a security process in which the user provides two different authentication factors to verify themselves. This typically involves something the user knows (a password) and something the user has (a token card or biometric), thereby providing a higher level of security than simple password protection.

4. **Answer:** A

Explanation: 'Least privilege' refers to the principle of providing users with the minimum levels of access, or permissions, required to perform their job functions. This security measure is intended to minimize the risk of accidental or intentional misuse of privileges.

5. **Answer:** B

Explanation: The primary purpose of a Business Continuity Plan (BCP) is to provide procedures for sustaining essential business operations while recovering from a significant disruption. This plan addresses business processes and the IT support required for those processes.

6. **Answer:** C

Explanation: The main difference between Business Continuity Planning (BCP) and Disaster Recovery Planning (DRP) is that BCP is a corporate requirement that addresses the continuation of business operations, whereas DRP is specifically focused on the IT recovery process and is considered an IT function.

7. **Answer:** D

Explanation: It is recommended that Business Continuity and Disaster Recovery plans be tested on a regular basis, not to exceed annually. For example, the Office of the Comptroller of the Currency (OCC) requires financial institutions to test their plans at least annually.

8. **Answer:** C

Explanation: The information security staff is responsible for establishing the security posture and strategy for various activities, including firewall administration, user account administration, anti-virus programs, encryption, and privacy compliance. Once in place, they ensure these processes are implemented as required.

9. **Answer:** D

Explanation: According to the text, an effective information security strategy requires four types of controls: preventive, detective, containment, and recovery. 'Enforcement' is not listed as one of the types of controls in the given strategy.

10. **Answer:** C

Explanation: A Service Level Agreement (SLA) is put in place to identify service levels, such as operational times, and recovery requirements, such as backup and restoration criteria. SLAs can be internal or with external third parties and are crucial when new applications, systems, or business processes move into production.

11. **Answer:** C

Explanation: BCP and DRP often fail because they have not been integrated as a business need and lack an internal risk assessment with the organization's stakeholders to understand the business reasons for implementing such plans.

12. **Answer:** D

Explanation: HIPAA, GLBA, and Sarbanes-Oxley are all mentioned as requirements to have a security program, whereas FCC is not listed in the provided context.

13. **Answer:** A

Explanation: The fiduciary duty assigned to management to protect the assets of the organization is made up of two key components: duty of loyalty and duty of care.

14. **Answer:** B

Explanation: Due diligence refers to the process of systematically evaluating information to identify risks and issues relating to a proposed transaction, ensuring that management makes informed business decisions.

15. **Answer:** B

Explanation: One of the ways senior management can openly demonstrate their support for the information security program is as simple as wearing their employee identification badges.

16. **Answer:** C

Explanation: Information security responsibilities should be defined in each employee's job description, and compliance with information security should be tied to an employee's performance-based objectives.

17. **Answer:** B

Explanation: The ISSC, made up of representatives from various business units, is the body responsible for championing and approving the policies, business continuity plan, and business impact analysis results, as required by law and international standards.

18. **Answer:** B

Explanation: The ultimate responsibility of senior management, from the context of a security program, is to assume the fiduciary duty to protect the assets of the organization, which includes information assets.

19. **Answer:** C

Explanation: Senior management needs to witness and demonstrate how the goals and objectives of the information security program will be met, which is part of their oversight responsibilities.

20. **Answer:** C

Explanation: Incorporating information security into the employee standards of conduct document is important because it discusses unacceptable activities and what will happen if employees are found to be in a noncompliant situation.

21. **Answer:** B

Explanation: Senior management is charged with the ultimate responsibility for meeting business objectives or mission requirements. They must ensure that necessary resources are effectively applied to develop capabilities to meet these requirements and incorporate risk assessment results into decision-making.

22. **Answer:** D

Explanation: CISO is responsible for the organization's planning, budgeting, and performance, including its information security components, and making decisions based on an effective risk management program.

23. **Answer:** C

Explanation: Information Owners as department managers assigned as functional owners of organization assets responsible for ensuring that proper controls are in place to address the integrity, confidentiality, and availability of the information resources they own.

24. **Answer:** B

Explanation: Business Managers, also known as owners, are responsible for making cost-benefit decisions essential to ensure the accomplishment of the organization's mission objectives and selecting business-oriented controls.

25. **Answer:** B

Explanation: employee compliance with security regulations, policies, and attitudes should be considered during the annual performance review process.

26. **Answer:** B

Explanation: Information security needs to work with human resources to make sure that security-related competencies for various job positions are defined, documented, and included in job descriptions.

27. **Answer:** B

Explanation: The asset classification policy must establish the term "owner" to refer to department managers who are responsible for the information resources.

28. **Answer:** C

Explanation: The Information Security Officer is the security program manager responsible for the organization's security programs, including risk management.

29. **Answer:** C

Explanation: The responsibility of serving as an "owner" aligns with the goal of fulfilling.

30. **Answer:** C

Explanation: Senior management must ensure that necessary resources are effectively applied to develop the capabilities needed to meet mission requirements.

31. **Answer:** C

Explanation: Management has the key responsibilities of fiduciary duty, which involves the obligation to act in the best interest of the organization, and due diligence, which requires taking the necessary steps to protect the company's information assets. These responsibilities are crucial for demonstrating compliance with legal and regulatory requirements and ensuring the success of an organization's security strategy.

32. **Answer:** B

Explanation: The main concern with information security reporting to operations is that the operations department must focus on completing production schedules and maintaining system availability for users. This priority might lead to necessary security controls being ignored or circumvented, as operations might overlook strict security measures that could interfere with productivity.

33. **Answer:** C

Explanation: In 2004, the National Cyber Security Summit Task Force published "Information Security Governance: A Call to Action." This document was a result of the work of the Corporate Governance Task Force, which was founded in 2003 to address the growing concerns regarding information security governance in organizations.

34. **Answer:** B

Explanation: The transition from centralized mainframe data centers to business unit workplaces with client/server open systems environments prompted internal auditing, the "Big 4" accounting firms, and security professionals to reassess the efficient location of information protection activity as information processing and storage became more decentralized.

35. **Answer:** D

Explanation: For information security to maintain a semblance of autonomy and be successful, it should report directly to the Chief Information Security Officer (CISO). This structure fosters the correct image of the information security function and promotes active partnerships within the organization.

36. **Answer:** C

Explanation: The primary responsibilities of the computer security group, , revolved around access control to the system and disaster recovery planning. This group's role is to ensure that data is protected and that there are plans in place to recover from potential disasters affecting the mainframe systems.

37. **Answer:** C

Explanation: In December 2005, the Cyber Security Industrial Alliance published its National Agenda for Information Security in 2006, recommending that the federal government "encourage" CEOs to review cyber security measures at board meetings. This initiative aimed to help senior executives understand the security-related implications of regulations such as Sarbanes-Oxley, GLBA, and HIPAA.

38. **Answer:** C

Explanation: Reporting information security to the auditing department would create a conflict of interest because it would mix the roles of those who make the rules (information security) with those who judge compliance (auditing). This could compromise the objectivity and independence necessary for effective auditing.

39. **Answer:** C

Explanation: The text indicates a significant change in focus, where information security is no longer viewed merely as a function of information technology. Instead, it is increasingly recognized as a critical business and governance issue that requires regular reporting to executive management and alignment with legal and regulatory requirements.

40. **Answer:** C

Explanation: It is crucial for senior management to support an information security program to demonstrate their compliance with key requirements such as fiduciary duty and due diligence. Senior management's commitment is essential for the success of the information security strategy, as they are responsible for approving policies, supporting them, and allocating sufficient funding.

41. **Answer:** B

Explanation: The primary goal of the Information Systems Security Association (ISSA) is to promote management practices that ensure the confidentiality, integrity, and availability of information resources. ISSA provides educational forums, publications, and opportunities for peer interaction to enhance the knowledge, skill, and professional growth of its members.

42. **Answer:** C

Explanation: Within an enterprise, the role of Information Security is to direct and support the company in protecting its information assets from intentional or unintentional disclosure, modification, destruction, or denial by implementing appropriate information security and business resumption planning policies, procedures, and guidelines.

43. **Answer:** C

Explanation: ISACA started as a group of individuals auditing controls in computer systems and has since become the world's leading membership organization for IT governance and control, offering centralized information, guidance, and education in the field.

44. **Answer:** B

Explanation: The annual report on the state of information security, typically prepared by the CISO, includes a report on the levels of compliance currently seen throughout the business units. It also includes the level of implementation for the current information security initiative, and it is distinct from a standard feature audit.

45. **Answer:** A

Explanation: A crucial element for the enterprise in making business decisions is implementing a formal risk analysis process to document all management decisions. This establishes accountability and due diligence, ensuring that decisions are based on the best needs of the enterprise and that prudent and reasonable controls are implemented.

46. **Answer:** A

Explanation: Information Protection is identified as a separate and distinct budget item within the overall Information Security Office (ISO) budget, typically allocated around 1-3% of the overall budget. This funding is dedicated to implementing and maintaining an effective IP program.

47. **Answer:** D

Explanation: The Information Protection (IP) program should be reviewed annually and modified where necessary to ensure its effectiveness and alignment with the evolving needs and objectives of the organization.

48. **Answer:** C

Explanation: ISACA was originally formed as the EDP Auditors Association in 1969. It started with a group of individuals focused on auditing controls in computer systems and now serves as a centralized source of information and guidance in the field.

49. **Answer:** D

Explanation: Published by the Computer Security Institute (CSI), the annual CSI/FBI Computer Crime and Security Survey aims to aggressively advocate the critical importance of protecting information assets by providing data on computer crime and security trends.

50. **Answer:** C

Explanation: The Chief Information Security Officer (CISO) is typically responsible for preparing the annual report on the state of information security. This report includes levels of compliance and the status of information security initiatives within the organization.

51. **Answer:** B

Explanation: The primary purpose of the GLBA is to provide privacy of customer information by financial service organizations and require comprehensive data protection measures.

52. **Answer:** B

Explanation: The Foreign Corrupt Practices Act (FCPA) requires companies to implement a due diligence program that includes a set of internal controls and enforcement to avoid liability.

53. **Answer:** B

Explanation: Fiduciary duty refers to the responsibility of management to protect the assets of the organization.

54. **Answer:** B

Explanation: The two important sections of the Sarbanes–Oxley Act (SOX) that have a meaningful impact on public companies and auditors are Sections 302 (Disclosure Controls and Procedures) and 404 (Internal Control Attest).

55. **Answer:** B

Explanation: Covered healthcare providers under HIPAA are required to use, disclose, and handle identifiable patient information according to strict privacy and security rules.

56. **Answer:** A

Explanation: One of the five keys of the information security program addressed in GLBA involves the Board of Directors, which includes reporting program effectiveness to them.

57. **Answer:** B

Explanation: The Federal Sentencing Guidelines require management to show "due diligence" by establishing policies, standards, and procedures to guide the workforce, among other actions.

58. **Answer:** A

Explanation: The Economic Espionage Act (EEA) of 1996 made trade secret theft a federal crime.

59. **Answer:** C

Explanation: The 'duty of care' refers to the duty of a director to discharge his/her duties in good faith, with care an ordinarily prudent person would exercise, and in a manner he/she reasonably believes is in the best interest of the enterprise.

60. **Answer:** B

Explanation: California legislation SB 1386 requires that if an incident occurs involving the compromise of personal information, the individuals whose personal information may have been compromised must be notified.

61. **Answer:** B

Explanation: An information security policy serves two primary roles: internally, it guides employees by setting expectations for their actions and how they will be judged; externally, it communicates to the world how the organization is managed and its commitment to asset protection.

62. **Answer:** B

Explanation: Security and privacy policies and procedures must be documented, communicated, and kept current to be effective.

63. **Answer:** B

Explanation: The three types of policies used in an information security program are Global (Tier 1), Topic-specific (Tier 2), and Application-specific (Tier 3).

64. **Answer:** B

Explanation: Senior management is responsible for issuing global policies (Tier 1) to establish the organization's direction in protecting information assets.

65. **Answer:** C

Explanation: Topic-specific policies (Tier 2) are often created or revised in response to relevant changes in technology or to comply with new laws.

66. **Answer:** C

Explanation: The Compliance or Consequences section spells out the consequences for non-compliance with the policy.

67. **Answer:** C

Explanation: Application-specific policies (Tier 3) focus on individual systems or applications.

68. **Answer:** B

Explanation: A policy should identify the appropriate contacts for additional information by job title, not individual name.

69. **Answer:** B

Explanation: Policies are generally brief and normally consist of one page of text using both sides of the paper.

70. **Answer:** C

Explanation: For a policy to be successfully reviewed and critiqued, it is important that it looks similar to other published policies from the organization, as some members of the review panel may struggle to engage with it otherwise.

71. **Answer:** C

Explanation: When developing procedures, it is recommended to use a technical writer to gather the relevant information from the SMEs. The technical writer should schedule an interview with the SMEs and request any written procedures they may have, along with any visual aids, to ensure that the information is translated accurately into the procedure format.

72. **Answer:** B

Explanation: The interview with the SME should be scheduled for 45 minutes. This duration is deemed sufficient to gather the necessary information without formalize on the SME's busy schedule.

73. **Answer:** B

Explanation: It is suggested that having teams develop procedures is not effective because it can slow down the process. This indicates that a more streamlined approach, possibly involving fewer people or more targeted expertise, is preferred for procedure development.

74. **Answer:** B

Explanation: After gathering all the necessary information from the SME, the next step is to put that information into a procedure format. This is part of the procedure writing process that involves drafting the procedure, reviewing and updating it based on feedback, and eventually publishing it.

75. **Answer:** C

Explanation: The SME is responsible for reviewing the draft procedure for content editing. This ensures that the procedure accurately reflects the specialized knowledge of the SME and is technically sound.

76. **Answer:** C

Explanation: The final step before publishing a procedure is to test it to ensure that it provides the proper results. This step is crucial to validate that the procedure works as intended before it is officially documented and disseminated.

77. **Answer:** D

Explanation: The procedure should be reviewed annually to ensure its continued relevance and effectiveness. Regular reviews help identify areas for improvement and update the procedure to reflect any changes in the work process or regulatory environment.

78. **Answer:** B

Explanation: After gathering information from the SME, the technical writer should inform both the SME and the SME backup about the next steps in the procedure writing process. This might include informing them when the draft procedure will be sent for their review and content editing.

79. **Answer:** C

Explanation: The SME backup is involved in reviewing the updated procedure for a final review, along with the SME. This ensures that more than one expert has validated the content and accuracy of the procedure before it is tested and published.

80. **Answer:** B

Explanation: The text indicates that, unlike policy development, procedures do not have to be approved by a management team. This suggests that the procedure approval process is less formal and does not necessarily involve team approvals, making the process quicker.

81. **Answer:** C

Explanation: Developing a business case for information security program investments is essential to justify funding. Organizations often base spending on the value a project brings to the enterprise, and the information security program, in particular, requires a strong business case to secure the necessary funding.

82. **Answer:** B

Explanation: The Company's market share is not mentioned as a factor affecting ROI in the text. The factors listed that affect the reliability of ROI as an indicator of corporate value include the length of project life, the capitalization policy, the rate at which depreciation is taken, the lag between investment outlays and the recouping of these outlays from cash inflows and the growth rate of new investment.

83. **Answer:** B

Explanation: TCO stands for Total Cost of Ownership, which is a financial estimate that helps assess both direct and indirect costs associated with the purchase of any capital investment, such as computer software or hardware.

This includes not just the purchase cost but also the costs of use and maintenance of the equipment or system.

84. **Answer:** C

Explanation: ROSI, or Return on Security Investment, calculates the economic value of a security investment. It factors in details such as risk management, reduction in perceived vulnerabilities, and loss of downtime, ultimately aiming to quantify the benefits of security measures.

85. **Answer:** B

Explanation: TCO includes a range of indirect costs, and some of the examples provided in the text are costs associated with failure or outage (planned and unplanned), diminished performance incidents, costs of security breaches (including loss of reputation and recovery costs), and more.

86. **Answer:** C

Explanation: Research groups at universities such as the University of Idaho, MIT, and Carnegie Mellon have developed robust and supportable data on Return on Security Investment (ROSI) calculations. This data and the resulting formulas can be integrated into business case models by information security managers to support investment decisions.

87. **Answer:** B

Explanation: The text highlights that the advancements in single sign-on and user access provisioning technologies have led to savings in time and cost compared to traditional manual administration techniques. These advancements can be used in the business case for most information security managers to justify investment in new security technologies.

88. **Answer:** A

Explanation: According to the text, the ROSI formula is represented as (R-E) + T = ALE, where T is the cost of the intrusion detection tool, E is the dollar savings gained by stopping intrusions through the tool, R is the cost per year to recover from intrusions, and ALE is the Annual Loss Expectancy.

89. **Answer:** B

Explanation: The ROI formula is considered unreliable for determining an information security program's success or corporate value because it may overstate the economic value. This overstatement depends on factors such as the length of project life, capitalization policy, depreciation rates, time lag between investment outlays and cash inflows, and the growth rate of new investment.

90. **Answer:** C

Explanation: The text mentions Return on Investment (ROI) and Total Cost of Ownership (TCO) as two common financial metrics used to justify spending on projects. ROI helps make capital investment decisions by considering the annual benefit compared to the investment amount, while TCO helps assess the direct and indirect costs related to the purchase and maintenance of an asset.

91. **Answer:** B

Explanation: The primary goal of risk management is to identify, control, and minimize the impact of uncertain events. It involves balancing protective measures' operational and economic costs while achieving gains in mission capability by safeguarding business processes. Risk management aims to reduce risks to an acceptable level, supporting senior management's due diligence.

92. **Answer:** A

Explanation: Risk analysis is a technique used to identify and assess factors that may jeopardize the success of a project or goal. It helps define preventive measures to reduce the likelihood of these factors occurring and identifies countermeasures to deal with these constraints if they develop.

93. **Answer:** C

Explanation: The text provides a formula for computing a single instance of risk within a system, which is (Asset * Threat * Vulnerability). This computation reflects how a threat exploiting a vulnerability can potentially cause harm to an asset.

94. **Answer:** B

Explanation: Vulnerability assessment and controls evaluation involve a systematic examination of critical infrastructure, interconnected systems, information, or products to determine the adequacy of security measures, identify security deficiencies, evaluate security alternatives, and verify the adequacy of such measures after their implementation.

95. **Answer:** C

Explanation: Risk assessment is the computation of risk, where risk is defined as a threat that exploits some vulnerability that could cause harm to an asset. The risk assessment process involves the algorithm that computes risk as a function of the assets, threats, and vulnerabilities.

96. **Answer:** C

Explanation: Risk mitigation is the process in which an organization implements controls and safeguards to prevent identified risks from

occurring. It also involves implementing means of recovery should the risk materialize despite all efforts to prevent it.

97. **Answer:** B

Explanation: Senior management of a department, business unit, group, or other such entity is considered to be the functional owner of the enterprise's assets. In their fiduciary duty, they act in the best interest of the enterprise to implement reasonable and prudent safeguards and controls.

98. **Answer:** B

Explanation: Senior management must ensure that the enterprise has the capabilities needed to accomplish its mission or business objectives. Risk management assists them in this task by providing tools to identify, assess, and mitigate risks that could hinder achieving these objectives.

99. **Answer:** B

Explanation: Senior management's support of the risk management process is a demonstration of their due diligence. It shows their commitment to protecting the assets of the organization by engaging in practices that identify, control, and minimize risks.

100. **Answer:** B

Explanation: In the context of calculating risk within a network, the total risk equates to the sum of all the individual risk instances. Each instance is computed using the formula (Asset * Threat * Vulnerability), and the total risk is the aggregation of these instances.

101. **Answer:** B

Explanation: The primary purpose of conducting a risk analysis, as stated in the text, is to document that "due diligence" has been performed during the decision-making process for new tasks or projects. This is essential for management to demonstrate they have responsibly considered potential risks before proceeding with an initiative.

102. **Answer:** C

Explanation: The Construction Phase is where the system or process is purchased, developed, or otherwise constructed. This is the phase where the actual building of the system takes place following the planning and design stages.

103. **Answer:** B

Explanation: The Chief Information Security Officer (CISO) is responsible for the organization's overall planning, budgeting, and performance, which includes the components related to information security. They make decisions based on an effective risk management program.

104. **Answer:** A

Explanation: According to the NIST, the first phase of the typical System Development Life Cycle (SDLC) is Initiation. This phase involves documenting the need for a new system, application, or process and its scope.

105. **Answer:** C

Explanation: Resource Owners are business unit managers responsible for the information resources they are assigned ownership of. They ensure that proper controls are in place to address the integrity, confidentiality, and availability of those resources.

106. **Answer:** C

Explanation: Once controls or safeguards have been implemented, a Network Vulnerability Assessment (NVA) should be conducted to determine if the controls are working as intended. This process assesses the effectiveness of existing controls, safeguards, and processes.

107. **Answer:** B

Explanation: The correct order of phases in the SDLC, as outlined by NIST, is Initiation, Development or Acquisition, Implementation, Operation or Maintenance, and Disposal.

108. **Answer:** B

Explanation: A risk analysis should be conducted before beginning any task, project, or development cycle to analyze the need for the project and to ensure that necessary spending is justified and risks are assessed.

109. **Answer:** B

Explanation: In information security, a vulnerability is defined as a condition where there is a missing or ineffectively administered safeguard or control, which allows a threat to occur with a greater impact or frequency, or both.

110. **Answer:** C

Explanation: The Information Security Professional is the program manager responsible for the organization's security programs, including risk management. This term has evolved from "officer" to avoid confusion with senior executive roles.

111. **Answer:** C

Explanation: The primary objective of conducting risk identification and analysis in a project is to identify and assess factors that may jeopardize a project's success or goal. This process is also known as a project impact analysis and includes a cost-benefit analysis to weigh the features, benefits, and costs associated with the project.

112. **Answer:** C

Explanation: It is important to consider the cost of not moving forward with a project because this decision can have a significant impact on the enterprise's competitive advantage, ability to meet its mission, and relationships with strategic business partners, suppliers, vendors, and other stakeholders. It also affects regulatory compliance issues and the overall strategic direction of the organization.

113. **Answer:** A

Explanation: The costs that must be factored into a project's risk analysis include procurement or development, operation, and maintenance costs. This includes expenses such as documentation development, user and infrastructure support training, possible upgrades, and conversion or migration costs, as well as their dollar values and staffing implications.

114. **Answer:** B

Explanation: A key deliverable from the asset definition step in the risk assessment process is a risk assessment statement of opportunity. This statement consists of two elements: a project statement and specifications, which define what the assessment will review and the expected outcomes.

115. **Answer:** C

Explanation: The purpose of threat identification during the risk assessment process is to create a complete list of potential threat sources that could affect the business objectives or mission of the business unit or enterprise. These threats can be natural, human, or environmental in nature.

116. **Answer:** D

Explanation: The three major categories of threat-sources identified in the risk assessment process are natural threats (such as floods and earthquakes), human threats (such as errors and deliberate acts such as fraud), and environmental threats (including long-term power outages and pollution). Astrological threats are not considered a category in this context.

117. **Answer:** A

Explanation: The correct sequence of steps in the risk assessment process includes Asset Definition, Threat Identification, Determine Probability of Occurrence, Determine the Impact of the Threat, Controls Recommended, and Documentation. This sequence ensures a thorough and systematic approach to assessing risk.

118. **Answer:** C

Explanation: When performing a cost-benefit analysis for new or enhanced controls, it is important to consider the cost of implementation, including initial outlay for hardware and software, reduction in operational effectiveness, additional policies and procedures, hiring or training staff, and ongoing maintenance costs. The analysis should determine if the control is cost-effective and appropriate for the organization.

119. **Answer:** B

Explanation: The methods of risk mitigation discussed in the text include Risk Assumption, Risk Alleviation, Risk Avoidance, Risk Limitation, Risk

Planning, and Risk Transference. Risk Augmentation is not mentioned as a method of risk mitigation.

120. **Answer:** C

Explanation: In the context of risk assessment, 'Risk Level' refers to the function of the probability that an identified threat will occur and then the impact that the threat will have on the business process or mission of the asset under review. Risk Level helps organizations prioritize threats and select appropriate controls to mitigate them.

121. **Answer:** C

Explanation: The primary goal of an effective risk assessment process is to align with the business objectives of the enterprise by identifying safeguards that meet its specific business needs. The process involves working with business owners to identify appropriate safeguards rather than enforcing security or audit requirements that may not align with the business's needs.

122. **Answer:** C

Explanation: Systems Management magazine reported that top IS project managers identified risk management as the number one functional capability they needed to be successful. This underscores the importance of managing risks effectively within projects to meet expectations and avoid negative consequences.

123. **Answer:** C

Explanation: When searching for threats during a risk assessment, three common sources should be considered: natural, human, and environmental. Human threats can be further divided into accidental and deliberate. These categories help teams consider a broad spectrum of potential threats that could impact the organization.

124. **Answer:** B

Explanation: The information security triad, which is a focal point during the risk assessment process, consists of integrity (protecting information from inappropriate modification or corruption), confidentiality (protecting information from unauthorized or accidental disclosure), and availability (ensuring authorized users can access applications and systems when required).

125. **Answer:** C

Explanation: The text describes using a threat occurrence rate table to establish the likelihood of a threat occurrence, which is then used to calculate the Annual Loss Exposure (ALE). This rate is determined by factors such as historical data and expert estimates to quantify the likelihood of threat events.

126. **Answer:** B

Explanation: When selecting controls and safeguards, it is important to consider their effectiveness, legal and regulatory requirements, and the operational impact on the organization. Popularity in the industry is not a recommended consideration, as the focus should be on the specific needs and compliance requirements of the enterprise.

127. **Answer:** C

Explanation: The value of a particular information resource must be determined by the business manager owner, and the process for classifying information must remain with the business unit. This cannot be discharged to the information security staff, audit, or any other third party. The classification policy must be tailored to the specific needs and sensitivity of the information resource.

128. **Answer:** A

Explanation: The first step in the risk assessment process is Threat Identification. After identifying the asset that needs protection, the process begins with looking for and identifying threats to those assets. This step is crucial for establishing the foundation of the risk assessment.

129. **Answer:** B

Explanation: In the context of information security, 'Loss of Integrity' refers to the requirement to protect information from improper modification. Integrity is lost if unauthorized changes are made to the data or the system, either intentionally or accidentally, which could lead to inaccuracy, fraud, or erroneous decisions.

130. **Answer:** B

Explanation: After identifying and consolidating threats, the risk assessment team is advised to establish a risk level for each threat. This involves assessing the probability of each threat occurring and its impact on the organization, then assigning an appropriate risk level to prioritize actions and resources.

131. **Answer:** C

Explanation: The primary role of the information security manager is to report significant changes in risk to appropriate levels of management on both a periodic and event-driven basis. This ensures management is aware of the current risk landscape and can make informed decisions.

132. **Answer:** C

Explanation: The risk assessment should be updated as changes occur within the organization to ensure it remains an accurate representation of the organization's risk profile.

133. **Answer:** C

Explanation: The periodic update meetings with upper management should include the status of the organization's overall security program, including any significant changes to the organization's risk profile.

134. **Answer:** C

Explanation: A significant security breach or security event should trigger a special report to upper management. This report should inform them of the event, its impact, and the steps being taken to mitigate the risk.

135. **Answer:** C

Explanation: A disadvantage of quantitative risk assessment is that the calculations are complex. It requires a good deal of preliminary work and historically works well only with recognized automated tools and associated knowledge bases.

136. **Answer:** C

Explanation: An advantage of qualitative risk assessment is that it's easier to involve non-security and non-technical staff, which can provide a broader perspective and help create a more comprehensive assessment.

137. **Answer:** B

Explanation: The disadvantage of qualitative risk assessment is that it is very subjective in nature, which can lead to varying interpretations and may

not provide a solid basis for a cost-benefit analysis of risk mitigation strategies.

138. **Answer:** B

Explanation: When reporting sensitive information to upper management, especially in the case of a special report due to a significant security breach or event, a secure channel should be utilized to prevent sensitive information from falling into the wrong hands.

139. **Answer:** D

Explanation: In qualitative risk assessment, it is not necessary to determine the dollar value of an asset because the assessment is based on subjective analysis rather than objective monetary measures.

140. **Answer:** B

Explanation: An information security manager should define processes for evaluating significant security events based on their impact on the organization. This allows them to determine the necessity of a special report and the appropriate steps to mitigate risk.

141. **Answer:** C

Explanation: Gap analysis is primarily utilized to measure the maturity level of an organization's security program. It involves assessing current security conditions against generally accepted practices or standards, such as ISO 17799:2000, to identify areas needing improvement and set targets for future enhancement.

142. **Answer:** B

Explanation: In order to determine Recovery Time Objectives (RTO), an organization must conduct a Business Impact Analysis (BIA). This analysis helps address all potential disasters, including sudden outages and rolling disasters and allows the organization to establish RTO and Recovery Point Objectives (RPO).

143. **Answer:** B

Explanation: The four essential aspects of information classification are:

(1) Information classification from a legal standpoint
(2) Responsibility for care and control of information
(3) Integrity of the information
(4) The criticality of the information and systems processing the information.

144. **Answer:** C

Explanation: The old concept in computer security was that everything is closed until it is opened, meaning that by default, information is not accessible until specific permissions are granted.

145. **Answer:** B

Explanation: It suggests keeping the number of information classification categories to as few as possible, typically three or four, to meet an organization's needs and avoid confusion.

146. **Answer:** B

Explanation: Classifying all information as 'confidential' would require special handling, which violates the concept of placing controls only where they are needed and leads to the misuse of limited resources.

147. **Answer:** C

Explanation: Organizations should avoid taking classification categories verbatim from another enterprise because each organization is unique. They should use information from other organizations as inspiration to create a set of categories and definitions that fit their specific needs.

148. **Answer:** B

Explanation: Classified information normally declines in sensitivity over time and should be automatically downgraded or declassified when it no longer meets the criteria established for such information.

149. **Answer:** B

Explanation: Part of an effective information classification program is to destroy documents when they are no longer required to ensure that the information is properly controlled and protected.

150. **Answer:** C

Explanation: Information classification drives the protection control requirements, allowing information to be protected to a level that matches its value to the organization. This helps eliminate the costs of overprotection and minimizes exceptions.

151. **Answer:** D

Explanation: The Physical Layer is the least complex layer in the OSI model, responsible for the mechanical, electrical, functional, and procedural standards to access the physical medium. It deals with the transmission of binary data (bits) over the network cable.

152. **Answer:** C

Explanation: The Data Link Layer sends information in the form of frames. This layer is responsible for transferring data between network entities and detecting and possibly correcting errors that may occur in the Physical Layer.

153. **Answer:** B

Explanation: The Network Layer provides administratively assigned addresses, such as IP addresses, and includes procedures for routing information through multiple networks.

154. **Answer:** C

Explanation: IP (Internet Protocol) is the most common Network Layer protocol, dealing with administratively assigned addresses and routing of information through multiple networks.

155. **Answer:** B

Explanation: The Transport Layer is responsible for several tasks, including flow control, windowing, data sequencing, and recovery.

156. **Answer:** B

Explanation: Switches operate at the Data Link Layer, providing functions and protocols to transfer data between network entities.

157. **Answer:** B

Explanation: The Session Layer provides mechanisms for organizing and structuring interaction between applications or devices and keeping multiple data streams separate.

158. **Answer:** C

Explanation: The Application Layer is the most complex and supports semantic exchanges between applications in open systems.

159. **Answer:** B

Explanation: Using DHCP poses a security risk because any system can plug into the network and immediately get a network address assigned, which an attacker could exploit.

160. **Answer:** C

Explanation: The Transport Layer is responsible for ensuring reliable end-to-end data transfer, which includes processes for resending information that was damaged or not received (error correction).

161. **Answer:** B

Explanation: The TCP/IP model provides the underlying architecture for many computer networks, including the Internet. It consists of a stack of four layers that define how data is transmitted across a network. This model is essential for enabling diverse systems to communicate with each other through standard protocols.

162. **Answer:** B

Explanation: The TCP/IP model is composed of four layers: Application, Transport (Host to Host), Internetwork (Internet), and Link (Network Interface). These layers work together to handle the transmission of data over the network.

163. **Answer:** A

Explanation: RFC 1149 is titled "A Standard for the Transmission of IP Datagrams on Avian Carriers." It describes an experimental method for data transmission using birds, which is not a practical or recommended standard but a humorous and well-known RFC.

164. **Answer:** B

Explanation: The subnet mask is used to distinguish the network portion of an IP address from the host portion. It is a binary mask with ones in the network part and zeros in the host part, which helps in determining the size of both the network and the host address spaces.

165. **Answer:** A

Explanation: Class A networks have the first byte in the range of 1 to 126. These networks can support a large number of hosts and have a network address with the leading bit set to 0, a 7-bit network number, and a 24-bit local host address.

166. **Answer:** C

Explanation: Class B networks can have approximately 65,000 hosts each. They are identified by a first byte range of 128 to 191 and have a network address with the two highest-order bits set to 1-0, a 14-bit network number, and a 16-bit local host address.

167. **Answer:** B

Explanation: RFC 2795, known as "The Infinite Monkey Protocol Suite (IMPS)," humorously describes a protocol suite that supports an infinite number of monkeys typing at an infinite number of typewriters. This is an example of an RFC that is not a serious technical standard.

168. **Answer:** B

Explanation: RFC 2324, the Hypertext Coffee Pot Control Protocol, is a humorous and fictional protocol and not actually related to information security. It describes a protocol for controlling coffee pots. RFCs 768, 1149, and 1918 are real standards, with the latter two being related to information security.

169. **Answer:** C

Explanation: The correct order of layers in the TCP/IP model from the highest (closest to the user) to the lowest (closest to the physical network) is: Application, Transport (Host to Host), Internetwork (Internet), and Link (Network Interface).

170. **Answer:** D

Explanation: Class D addresses are designated for multicast traffic. They are not used for standard host-to-host communication. Multicast addresses are used to deliver packets to a group of destinations rather than a single destination.

171. **Answer:** B

Explanation: The Time to Live (TTL) field in an IP datagram header is used to specify the duration a datagram can exist on the network. It is a mechanism that limits the lifespan or transit time of data in a network. The TTL value is set initially by the sender, and it is decremented by each router through which the datagram passes. If the TTL reaches zero before the datagram reaches its destination, the datagram is discarded, and an error message is sent back to the sender. This prevents datagrams from circulating indefinitely and potentially creating network congestion.

172. **Answer:** C

Explanation: Network Address Translation (NAT) is used to conserve the limited number of available public IP addresses and to provide a form of security by hiding an organization's internal IP addresses. NAT allows devices with private IP addresses to communicate with the Internet by translating their private addresses to public address. It does not inherently increase the speed of the Internet connection.

173. **Answer:** A

Explanation: The "24-bit block" refers to the private IP address range of 10.0.0.0–10.255.255.255, also known as the 10/8 prefix. This block is a single class A network number that can be used within an organization without the risk of address conflict with devices on the public Internet.

174. **Answer:** B

Explanation: The Header Checksum field in the IP datagram header is used to protect the header against errors that might occur during transmission. It is a form of error-checking that allows the receiving node to detect any corruption of the header data. The sending node calculates the checksum based on the header contents before sending the datagram, and the receiving node recalculates it upon arrival to verify the integrity of the header.

175. **Answer:** D

Explanation: The IP address 203.49.27.136 is considered a public IP address because it does not fall within any of the private IP address ranges specified by the Internet Assigned Numbers Authority (IANA). The other options (A, B, and C) represent addresses within the private ranges and are not valid for use on the public Internet.

176. **Answer:** B

Explanation: The "16-bit block" of private IP addresses is a set of 256 contiguous class C network numbers, represented by the range 192.168.0.0–192.168.255.255, also known as the 192.168/16 prefix.

177. **Answer:** C

Explanation: The Fragment Offset field in the IP datagram header is used to specify the position of a fragment in a fragmented datagram. It allows for the proper reassembly of the original datagram by indicating where in the sequence the fragment belongs.

178. **Answer:** B

Explanation: The Protocol field in the IP datagram header indicates the upper layer protocol to which the data portion of the datagram should be passed at the destination. This field ensures that the payload is directed to the correct process, such as TCP (Protocol 6) or UDP (Protocol 17).

179. **Answer:** D

Explanation: Network Address Translation (NAT) is typically performed by devices that route traffic between networks, such as firewalls, layer three switches, routers, proxies, and cable/DSL modems. A Network Attached Storage (NAS) device is used for data storage and is not involved in the translation of network addresses.

180. **Answer:** D

Explanation: All of the listed IP address ranges (10.0.0.0–10.255.255.255, 172.16.0.0–172.31.255.255, 192.168.0.0–192.168.255.255) are reserved for private use and can be used by Category 1 hosts that do not require access to hosts in other enterprises or the Internet at large. These addresses are

unambiguous within an enterprise but may be ambiguous between enterprises.

181. **Answer:** B

Explanation: TCP is a connection-oriented, stateful protocol that establishes a connection between a source and destination to provide reliable communication and error recovery. It ensures data is sent and received correctly, and it provides mechanisms like flow control to manage the rate of data transmission.

182. **Answer:** B

Explanation: The well-known port numbers range from 0 to 1023 and are reserved for assignment by the Internet Corporation for Assigned Names and Numbers (ICANN) for the most prevalent services on the Internet, like HTTP, FTP, and email.

183. **Answer:** C

Explanation: Port number 80 is commonly used for HTTP traffic, which is the protocol used to transfer web pages on the Internet.

184. **Answer:** B

Explanation: In the context of computer networking, a port serves as a memory address space that allows a single host to run multiple services, each identified by a unique port number, similar to phone extensions within a company.

185. **Answer:** C

Explanation: Both TCP and UDP have separate memory address spaces ranging from 0 to 65,535, which allows two applications to run on the same port number as long as they use different protocols (TCP or UDP).

186. **Answer:** C

Explanation: A closed port response during a port scan means that the port is not open for connections. The host is reachable, but the application associated with the port is not actively listening for connections.

187. **Answer:** C

Explanation: The SYN flag in the TCP header is used to initiate a TCP connection between two systems. It begins the process of synchronizing sequence numbers, which is essential for establishing a reliable connection.

188. **Answer:** C

Explanation: The Window field in the TCP header informs the sender of the rate at which packets can be sent based on the receiver's ability to process the incoming data. It is a crucial aspect of TCP's flow control mechanism.

189. **Answer:** C

Explanation: Common responses to a port scan include open (allowing communication), closed (responding with a port closed response), and filtered (no response, typically indicating a firewall is blocking the request).

190. **Answer:** B

Explanation: The Checksum field in the TCP header is used as an error-checking mechanism. It verifies the integrity of the TCP header and portions of the IP header, helping to detect any corruption in the transmitted data.

191. **Answer:** C

Explanation: The SYN flag is used in the first step of the TCP three-way handshake to synchronize sequence numbers between the client and the server. Each party sends a packet with the SYN flag set containing its initial sequence number (ISN) to establish a unique sequence number for the session.

192. **Answer:** D

Explanation: Each TCP connection uses a pseudorandom ISN to prevent packets from different connections from being confused with each other and to reduce predictability, which could be exploited by attackers.

193. **Answer:** D

Explanation: After receiving Sally's SYN packet, Bob responds with a SYN-ACK packet. This packet contains Bob's own ISN and acknowledges the receipt of Sally's ISN.

194. **Answer:** B

Explanation: The ACK packet is sent by the client in response to the server's SYN-ACK packet. This finalizes the three-way handshake and signifies that both parties have received each other's ISN and are ready to transfer data.

195. **Answer:** B

Explanation: The correct order of the TCP three-way handshake is, the client sends a SYN packet, the server responds with a SYN-ACK packet, and the client replies with an ACK packet.

196. **Answer:** C

Explanation: A timed counter that is incremented every four microseconds was traditionally used to generate a unique ISN. Most implementations now use more complex algorithms to select pseudorandom ISNs to prevent conflicts and improve security.

197. **Answer:** C

Explanation: Sally sends a packet with the FIN flag set to Bob to gracefully close the connection, indicating that the communication is done and the connection can be closed.

198. **Answer:** B

Explanation: In contract to, TCP, which is connection-oriented, UDP is a connectionless protocol. It does not establish a connection before sending data and does not guarantee delivery or order of packets.

199. **Answer:** C

Explanation: Applications may choose UDP over TCP when speed is more important than reliability. UDP has minimal overhead due to the absence of flags, states, sequence numbers, or acknowledgment numbers.

200. **Answer:** B

Explanation: Since UDP does not have a way to send a reset (RST) packet as TCP does, it responds to packets addressed to a closed port with an ICMP

error message. This is an example of one protocol (UDP) using another protocol (ICMP) for communication.

201. **Answer:** C

Explanation: ICMP is designed primarily to help troubleshoot networks by carrying out error reporting. It works alongside IP to inform the sending station when packets, especially UDP packets, do not reach their destination.

202. **Answer:** B

Explanation: ICMP is a transport-layer protocol such as TCP and UDP, and it follows the IP header in a normal packet structure to perform its error reporting and diagnostic functions

203. **Answer:** B

Explanation: The Type field in the ICMP header is 8 bits in length and it defines the type of ICMP message, which indicates the purpose of the message.

204. **Answer:** B

Explanation: In a Type 3 ICMP message ("Destination unreachable"), a Code value of 0 means "Network unreachable," which implies a router failure.

205. **Answer:** C

Explanation: An ICMP Type 8 message is known as an echo request, which is used by the ping command to test connectivity between hosts.

206. **Answer:** B

Explanation: The checksum field is used for error checking and is calculated in the same way as the IP header checksum to ensure the integrity of the ICMP message.

207. **Answer:** C

Explanation: Typically, the data portion of an ICMP packet includes the IP header and the first 64 bits of the original packet, which allows the ICMP message to be matched to the packet that triggered it.

208. **Answer:** B

Explanation: A Type 3 ICMP packet corresponds to a "Destination unreachable" message, which is used when a router cannot forward a packet to the next hop, often due to security devices such as firewalls.

209. **Answer:** B

Explanation: The trace route sends a series of IP packets with incrementing TTL values to discover the routers along the path to a destination by eliciting ICMP "time exceeded" messages from each router.

210. **Answer:** D

Explanation: IP and related protocols, such as ICMP, were designed for interoperability and redundancy, not for security, which makes them susceptible to various types of attacks.

211. **Answer:** C

Explanation: The primary goal of information security, as illustrated by the CIA Triad, is to protect the accuracy, confidentiality, and availability of

information. These are the three primary tenets that ensure information is correct (integrity), restricted to authorized individuals (confidentiality), and accessible when needed (availability).

212. **Answer:** B

Explanation: Integrity, as defined by ISO 17799 within information security, refers to the action of safeguarding the accuracy and completeness of information and processing methods, ensuring that when a user requests information, it is correct and has not been tampered with.

213. **Answer:** B

Explanation: According to linux.org, the acronym RAID stands for Redundant Array of Inexpensive Disks. This technology allows a system to maintain data even in the event of a hard-drive crash through various configurations such as disk mirroring, disk duplexing, and more complex solutions such as RAID 5.

214. **Answer:** D

Explanation: RAID 10 combines the techniques of mirroring (RAID 1) and striping (RAID 0). This configuration provides both performance benefits from striping and redundancy from mirroring, allowing it to support multiple drive failures.

215. **Answer:** C

Explanation: A UPS, or Uninterruptible Power Supply, is a device that helps maintain the availability of a system in the event of a power failure. It can also provide the integrity of the data by allowing the system to shut down gracefully if power is lost for an extended period of time.

216. **Answer:** A

Explanation: The PPPN model used by the ISACA organization as part of the CISM certification breaks down into four components: Process, Physical, Platform, and Network. Each component represents a different set of controls that can be used to enhance the integrity, confidentiality, and availability of data within an organization.

217. **Answer:** C

Explanation: Platform controls are those that verify the confidentiality, integrity, and authenticity of a single device or host. Operating system security controls fall under this category because they protect the system at the host level, in contract to firewalls and intrusion detection systems, which are considered network controls, and visitor badges, which are physical controls.

218. **Answer:** C

Explanation: Process controls within the PPPN model include policies, procedures, and guidelines that address the confidentiality, integrity, and availability of all systems in an organization. These are foundational and drive the information security program, unlike RAID configurations (platform), virus detection software (platform), and biometric access systems (physical).

219. **Answer:** A

Explanation: The disadvantage of using RAID systems is that you lose some of the storage space from the devices to maintain redundancy or parity. For instance, a RAID 5 configuration with five 80-gigabyte hard drives would only offer 320 gigabytes of actual storage space due to parity data storage.

220. **Answer:** D

Explanation: System failover technology involves setting up a secondary system that automatically takes over processing in the event that the primary system experiences a hardware failure. This helps to maintain availability without a single point of failure, which is especially common in firewall configurations to prevent network outages.

221. **Answer:** C

Explanation: Crackers break into systems with malicious intent, often seeking to damage or destroy data. Unlike hackers, who might be motivated by the desire to improve security and inform administrators of vulnerabilities, crackers have no such etiquette and aim to cause disruption.

222. **Answer:** C

Explanation: Attackers often maintain access to a compromised server by uploading custom applications or backdoors. These allow them to re-enter the system at will without detection.

223. **Answer:** D

Explanation: During the Covering Tracks phase, attackers attempt to erase evidence of their activities from system logs to avoid detection by system administrators or during a forensic examination.

224. **Answer:** C

Explanation: Trojan horses appear to be legitimate software but conceal malicious code. They can be deceptive and are often used to trick users into running them, believing they serve a useful purpose.

225. **Answer:** C

Explanation: A logic bomb is a type of malicious code that lies dormant until a specific trigger event occurs, such as a date or an action, at which point it executes its malicious payload.

226. **Answer:** A

Explanation: DDoS attacks are characterized by the use of multiple compromised systems (zombie hosts) to attack a single target, making it a many-to-one attack rather than a one-to-one attack.

227. **Answer:** B

Explanation: The first phase is Reconnaissance, where the attacker gathers information about the target through passive and active means to identify vulnerabilities and plan the attack.

228. **Answer:** C

Explanation: A rootkit is a collection of software tools that gives an attacker the ability to replace essential system files with Trojanized versions, allowing for persistent and stealthy access to the system.

229. **Answer:** B

Explanation: A virus attaches itself to files and spreads when those files are accessed, whereas a worm is a self-contained program that replicates itself to spread to other systems without needing to attach to other files.

230. **Answer:** C

Explanation: A Denial-of-Service (DoS) attack aims to make a network or system resources unavailable to its intended users by overwhelming the system's hardware resources or its network bandwidth.

231. **Answer:** B

Explanation: Social engineering attacks aim to manipulate individuals into divulging confidential information that can be used for unauthorized access or theft. Social engineers exploit human tendencies such as the desire to be helpful, trust in others, the fear of getting into trouble, and a willingness to cut corners to achieve this goal.

232. **Answer:** D

Explanation: Social engineers exploit human nature, such as the desire to be helpful, a tendency to trust easily, and the fear of getting into trouble. They do not exploit an inclination to follow strict security procedures; in fact, they take advantage of the opposite behavior.

233. **Answer:** C

Explanation: A dictionary attack is a technique used by hackers where they utilize a dictionary of common passwords to quickly guess and break into accounts with weak password security. It is effective because many users choose simple passwords that are easy to guess.

234. **Answer:** D

Explanation: Brute force attack: Tries every single combination of characters possible until the password is cracked. This is slow and inefficient.

Dictionary attack: Uses a list of common passwords, phrases, and combinations to try guessing the password. This is faster and leverages the fact that many people use weak passwords.

235. **Answer:** C

Explanation: A Man-in-the-Middle (MITM) attack is a security breach where the attacker secretly intercepts and possibly alters the communication between two parties who believe they are directly communicating with each other. The attacker can then steal or manipulate the data being exchanged.

236. **Answer:** B

Explanation: Mandatory Access Control (MAC) is a system where access permissions are determined by a strict policy, often used by organizations with high-security standards, such as government agencies. It requires the classification of every person, document, and system, with access permissions set through background checks, need to know, and security classification levels.

237. **Answer:** B

Explanation: Discretionary Access Control (DAC) allows permissions to be assigned by data custodians or administrators based on the user's job function. It is less costly and has less administrative overhead compared to MAC, and its flexibility is advantageous for organizations with rapidly changing environments.

238. **Answer:** C

Explanation: Organizations may opt for DAC over MAC because it is less expensive due to reduced administrative overhead, and it offers more flexibility, making it suitable for environments that experience frequent changes. DAC allows permissions to be granted based on job roles and is more adaptable to organizational changes compared to the more rigid MAC framework.

239. **Answer:** C

Explanation: The main disadvantage of DAC is that its flexibility can lead to security breaches over time, as permissions can be modified, potentially leading to less stringent security. DAC does not require the extensive classification of documents and users such as MAC, but this can also make it more vulnerable to security lapses.

240. **Answer:** D

Explanation: An advantage of MAC is that it typically provides greater security than DAC. Security in MAC is determined by a strict policy, and changes in permissions require policy modifications. This rigidity helps to maintain a high level of security, which is why it is often implemented in organizations with stringent security requirements.

241. **Answer:** B

Explanation: The primary goal of access control is to create nonrepudiation, which means ensuring that a userID is tied without any chance of compromise with one person. Nonrepudiation ensures that if a message is generated from a user's e-mail account, it is indeed sent by that user.

242. **Answer:** C

Explanation: Knowledge-based authentication methods rely on something the user knows, such as passwords or Personal Identification Numbers (PINs).

243. **Answer:** B

Explanation: A lattice-based access control system lays out users and files to define relationships between the access permissions, allowing an information security manager to identify security violations and areas needing more security.

244. **Answer:** C

Explanation: The major drawback of script-based SSO is that passwords are typically stored in plaintext and transmitted over the network in plaintext, which can be easily intercepted by attackers using network sniffers.

245. **Answer:** B

Explanation: In RBAC, permissions are assigned to job functions. Users are then assigned to these job functions, which is particularly useful in roles with high employee turnover, such as help desk positions.

246. **Answer:** C

Explanation: Token-based authentication is beneficial because it adds complexity to the authentication process, which helps mitigate the risk associated with weak passwords.

247. **Answer:** B

Explanation: The three ways a user can authenticate to access control systems are knowledge-based (like passwords or PINs), characteristics-based (such as biometrics), and possession-based (including tokens and tickets).

248. **Answer:** B

Explanation: Two-factor authentication improves security by requiring authentication methods from two different categories: something you know, something you have, or something you are.

249. **Answer:** B

Explanation: One-time passwords are effective in mitigating the risk of network sniffer attacks because they are valid for only one login, making it difficult for attackers to reuse captured credentials.

250. **Answer:** B

Explanation: Access control lists are used by devices such as firewalls and routers to define who can access those systems or which types of data can bypass these systems, often based on specific rules such as IP addresses.

251. **Answer:** D

Explanation: RADIUS is commonly used as the back-end authentication mechanism for 802.1x networks, which allows for dynamic password use and is compatible with newer wireless network authentication schemes.

252. **Answer:** C

Explanation: RADIUS uses UDP (User Datagram Protocol) as its transport-layer protocol, which is not connection-oriented, meaning that authentication packets can potentially be lost without the client being made aware.

253. **Answer:** B

Explanation: Diameter is the protocol proposed to replace RADIUS, and it uses TCP (Transmission Control Protocol) for greater reliability in authentication processes.

254. **Answer:** A

Explanation: TACACS stands for Terminal Access Controller Access-Control System, and TACACS+ is a more advanced version with increased authentication options.

255. **Answer:** C

Explanation: 802.1x and EAP provide dynamic authentication and configuration features, including IP address assignment and VLAN setup, but they cannot enforce a security policy on the entire Internet.

256. **Answer:** B

Explanation: EAP, or Extensible Authentication Protocol, works with 802.1x to provide extensible user-based authentication, which changes the role of authentication from the machine to the user.

257. **Answer:** B

Explanation: A physical zone of control refers to a physical area, such as the fourth floor of an office building, for which an information security manager sets the security policy.

258. **Answer:** C

Explanation: A firewall's main purpose is to enforce security policy by segmenting the network into trusted and untrusted zones, requiring users to pass through the firewall's policy to access different segments.

259. **Answer:** C

Explanation: For a communication to be considered inside the zone of control, both the sender and receiver must be located within the designated physical or logical zone.

260. **Answer:** B

Explanation: The 802.1x standard provides extensible authentication through the Extensible Authentication Protocol (EAP) for dynamic environments such as educational institutions where network users may change locations frequently.

261. **Answer:** C

Explanation: Proxy-based firewalls operate at the application layer of the OSI model. They are capable of filtering decisions based on in-depth packet information, which theoretically makes them more secure but also slower and more expensive compared to other types of firewalls.

262. **Answer:** B

Explanation: Stateful inspection firewalls use a dynamic database to track connection states, thus requiring only two rules for a configuration that would take four rules in a packet filter firewall. This is achieved by dynamically creating rules for responses to outbound requests.

263. **Answer:** C

Explanation: Packet filter firewalls are criticized for having major security concerns related to the large number of ports that remain open for unsolicited Internet traffic, which could lead to security breaches.

264. **Answer:** B

Explanation: Stateful inspection firewalls build a dynamic database that monitors the state of connections, allowing them to dynamically manage rules and mitigate some of the exposures of packet filter firewalls.

265. **Answer:** B

Explanation: Packet filter firewalls are known for their speed because they examine minimal data within packets to make filtering decisions, focusing on source and destination addresses and ports.

266. **Answer:** C

Explanation: Proxy-based firewalls do not support custom applications well, as they require custom-written code to understand and properly filter the application data.

267. **Answer:** B

Explanation: Stateful inspection firewalls can be susceptible to spoofing attacks where attackers create fraudulent packets that trick the firewall into opening dynamic rules that allow the attacker's traffic.

268. **Answer:** C

Explanation: VLANs, or Virtual Local Area Networks, are used to create network segmentation or subdomain isolation, effectively dividing a physical network into separate logical segments that limit network traffic between segments.

269. **Answer:** D

Explanation: While proxy-based firewalls tend to be more expensive due to their deeper inspection capabilities, stateful inspection firewalls can also be relatively costly, especially higher-end models.

270. **Answer:** A

Explanation: Packet filter firewalls are sometimes included for free with the purchase of other network devices like low-end cable modems, DSL routers, and wireless access points due to their basic level of security.

271. **Answer:** C

Explanation: The primary disadvantage of using physical distance, or creating an air gap, for segmentation, is that it offers minimal security. If someone inadvertently connects the physically separated networks, the security is compromised.

272. **Answer:** C

Explanation: Subnetting isolates networks by assigning two different IP address ranges to separate networks, preventing them from communicating with each other.

273. **Answer:** C

Explanation: NIDS are becoming less effective mainly because the encryption used to protect network communication and attacks makes it difficult for NIDS to distinguish between normal traffic and attack traffic.

274. **Answer:** B

Explanation: Anomaly identification systems can report legitimate traffic as inappropriate if the traffic deviates from established baselines or RFC standards, which may occur with new applications that do not comply.

275. **Answer:** C

Explanation: A router creates segmentation by blocking communication between network segments through Access Control Lists (ACLs), which are rules that dictate traffic flow.

276. **Answer:** D

Explanation: According to the text, a firewall is the most secure method of segmentation or subdomain isolation, although it is also the most expensive.

277. **Answer:** C

Explanation: The text states that about 70 percent of intrusions come from internal sources, highlighting the risk posed by employees within an organization.

278. **Answer:** C

Explanation: Automated IDS responses can be exploited by attackers who spoof packets to include known attacks, thereby tricking the IDS into blocking legitimate traffic and causing a denial-of-service attack.

279. **Answer:** C

Explanation: Tripwire is mentioned as an example of a host-based intrusion detection system that monitors file integrity to ensure critical system files are not modified.

280. **Answer:** B

Explanation: The main disadvantage of a manual response to IDS alerts is operator inattention, which can occur due to the number of false positives generated by the system, potentially allowing attacks to continue if alerts are ignored.

281. **Answer:** C

Explanation: The third generation of IDS systems is considered to be Intrusion Prevention Systems (IPS), which are intended to encompass intrusion detection, vulnerability assessment, anti-virus, and firewall technologies all in one.

282. **Answer:** B

Explanation: In cryptography, the CIA triad stands for Confidentiality, Integrity, and Authenticity, unlike the standard CIA triad, which stands for Confidentiality, Integrity, and Availability.

283. **Answer:** C

Explanation: The primary goal of cryptography is secrecy, which originates from its use in military operations to exchange information without the enemy being able to intercept and read the communication.

284. **Answer:** B

Explanation: Nonrepudiation of origin is a cryptographic principle that guarantees the authenticity and integrity of a message, ensuring that the sender is genuine and the message has not been altered.

285. **Answer:** B

Explanation: Key escrow involves storing a copy of a cryptographic key with a trusted third party, allowing encrypted data to be accessed in situations where the original key is lost or unavailable.

286. **Answer:** C

Explanation: The work factor is the measure of the time, effort, and resources that would be necessary to break the cryptosystem without having the appropriate key.

287. **Answer:** B

Explanation: Ciphertext refers to the data that has been encrypted and is unreadable to anyone except the intended recipient who has the key to decrypt it.

288. **Answer:** B

Explanation: Kerckhoff's Principle states that the security of a cryptosystem should depend only on the secrecy of the key, not on the secrecy of the algorithm, which should be publicly known.

289. **Answer:** C

Explanation: Deciphering is the process of converting ciphertext back into its original readable form, known as plaintext.

290. **Answer:** C

Explanation: Key clustering is a method that allows another key, apart from the original, to be used to decrypt the encrypted data. This can be useful for data recovery in case the original key is lost.

291. **Answer:** B

Explanation: Private key cryptography does not scale well to large numbers of users because the number of key pairs that need to be managed grows large quickly. Each user requires a unique key shared with every other user, leading to a combinatorial explosion in the number of keys.

292. **Answer:** B

Explanation: The most common ways for private keys to be exchanged include insecure methods such as email and fax, presenting a significant security risk as these channels are susceptible to interception.

293. **Answer:** B

Explanation: Private keys that are generated by humans tend to be weak because they are short, based on dictionary words, and contain only letters and numbers, which makes them easier to guess or brute force.

294. **Answer:** C

Explanation: Triple-DES, which encrypts a message three times using the DES algorithm, is considered a legacy cryptosystem because it is slow and has been largely replaced by the more modern and secure Advanced Encryption Standard (AES).

295. **Answer:** D

Explanation: The major issue with the clipper chip, which was intended to implement the Skipjack algorithm in secure hardware, was a government backdoor that led to public outcry and ultimately forced the government to stop supporting the chip.

296. **Answer:** D

Explanation: Output Feedback Mode (OFB) is the mode of DES operation that functions as a stream cipher, using a key stream generator and exclusively ORing the plaintext before encrypting the message with the normal DES process.

297. **Answer:** A

Explanation: Public key cryptography is based on the mathematical challenge of factoring very large prime numbers that have been multiplied together, which is a difficult problem that provides the security of the cryptographic system.

298. **Answer:** B

Explanation: Public key cryptography allows for better scalability because it does not require shared keys among users and can handle a large number of users more efficiently, with administration becoming easier once the initial setup is complete.

299. **Answer:** A

Explanation: The certificate revocation list is used in public key cryptography to list keys that have been compromised or are no longer valid, effectively revoking the associated certificates and preventing the use of the listed keys.

300. **Answer:** C

Explanation: The Rijndael algorithm, created by two Belgians, was selected for the Advanced Encryption Standard (AES) because of its complexity and speed, and after extensive public review and testing, it became the chosen standard.

301. **Answer:** B

Explanation: The primary purpose of a stream cipher is to encrypt data by processing the message bit by bit, using a key stream generator to produce a stream of random bits that gets XORed with the plaintext.

302. **Answer:** B

Explanation: A keystream generator must have long periods where the key stream does not repeat to ensure security. Therefore, it should not repeat after short periods.

303. **Answer:** C

Explanation: The encryption protocol Wired Equivalent Privacy (WEP) used by wireless networks employs a stream cipher called RC4.

304. **Answer:** B

Explanation: An Initialization Vector (IV) is used to prevent defining a relationship between the plaintext and the ciphertext, making encrypted messages appear unique.

305. **Answer:** D

Explanation: Cipher Block Chaining (CBC) involves using part of the previous message's ciphertext to combine with the key to create a more random-appearing key for the next message.

306. **Answer:** C

Explanation: The most common type of cryptanalysis attack is the ciphertext-only attack, where an attacker analyzes the encrypted messages to search for patterns.

307. **Answer:** D

Explanation: Symmetric encryption is a method of cryptography, not cryptanalysis. The other options are actual cryptanalysis methods.

308. **Answer:** C

Explanation: The primary goal of a digital signature is to authenticate the sender and verify that the message has not been modified, ensuring non-repudiation.

309. **Answer:** D

Explanation: The MD5 algorithm is mentioned as generating a 128-bit electronic fingerprint or hash.

310. **Answer:** B

Explanation: Hash functions such as MD5 and SHA are used to create an electronic fingerprint of data, allowing verification of the integrity of the information.

311. **Answer:** D

Explanation: A substitution cipher replaces one letter from the plaintext message with another character to encrypt the message. The Caesar cipher is an example of a substitution cipher where letters are shifted a certain number of places down the alphabet.

312. **Answer:** C

Explanation: The Caesar cipher encrypts a message by shifting the alphabet by a set number of spaces to substitute letters in the plaintext message.

313. **Answer:** B

Explanation: Substitution ciphers change one letter for another, while transposition ciphers change the sequence of the letters in the message.

314. **Answer:** A

Explanation: A poly-alphabetic cipher uses multiple alphabets to encrypt a message. The Caesar cipher is considered a poly-alphabetic cipher because it switches from the standard alphabet to a shifted one.

315. **Answer:** B

Explanation: A running key cipher uses a pre-agreed set of characters where each character or number represents a specific part of the message.

316. **Answer:** A

Explanation: Steganography involves hiding messages within the least significant bits of digital files, such as photos or music files so that the presence of the message is not apparent.

317. **Answer:** B

Explanation: Steganography hides a message in such a way that it is not obvious a message is being sent, while cryptography involves encrypting messages that can be detected but not easily deciphered.

318. **Answer:** B

Explanation: Pig Latin is an example of a code where a system is agreed upon to hide the meaning of messages.

319. **Answer:** C

Explanation: The Enigma machine was an encryption device that used rotors and switches to encrypt messages; it was famously used by the Nazis during World War II.

320. **Answer:** D

Explanation: A transposition cipher involves changing the sequence of letters in the message. Writing the letters of a word in reverse order is a simple form of a transposition cipher.

321. **Answer:** C

Explanation: The primary purpose of the initial key exchange in an SSL session is to securely exchange a session key using public key encryption. This session key is then used for symmetric encryption for the rest of the communication, balancing security with speed.

322. **Answer:** A

Explanation: A cipher suite is a combination of algorithms used during the SSL/TLS handshake process, and it typically includes the protocol version, an encryption algorithm, and a hash function. The session key is generated during the handshake process but is not a component of the cipher suite itself.

323. **Answer:** C

Explanation: A Certificate Authority (CA) is responsible for signing digital certificates. These certificates are used in the SSL handshake to verify the identity of the server and establish trust between the server and the client.

324. **Answer:** B

Explanation: After the server sends its digital certificate, the client checks if the Certificate Authority (CA) that signed the digital certificate is in the browser's trusted list. If the CA is trusted and other checks pass, the certificate is accepted for further processing.

325. **Answer:** B

Explanation: A Message Authentication Code (MAC) uses symmetric cryptography to verify both the integrity and authenticity of a message. Unlike a digital signature, it does not authenticate an individual but authenticates all parties to a conversation.

326. **Answer:** B

Explanation: Encapsulated Secure Payload (ESP) is a component of IPSEC that is responsible for encrypting the data portion of packets to protect the information in transit over the network, ensuring confidentiality.

327. **Answer:** B

Explanation: A risk table such as the one described in the context is used to classify risks into high, medium, and low categories based on their likelihood of occurrence and potential impact on the organization.

328. **Answer:** B

Explanation: Baselines are sets of minimum controls that are applied to systems that do not contain highly sensitive information. They provide a basic level of security and establish a guideline for best practices.

329. **Answer:** C

Explanation: Within a Public Key Infrastructure (PKI), a Certificate Authority (CA) is responsible for publishing public keys. This enables users to access public keys to verify corresponding private keys and establish secure communications.

330. **Answer:** C

Explanation: The Authentication Header (AH) in IPSEC is used to authenticate IP packets and ensure their integrity. It provides a way to verify that the packets are from a legitimate source and have not been tampered with, using a Security Associate (SA) and Security Parameter Index (SPI).

331. **Answer:** B

Explanation: The 802.11b standard operates on the 2.4 GHz frequency band. This is different from the 802.11a standard, which operates at 5 GHz and significantly higher than the frequency used by normal walkie-talkies, which operate at 49 MHz.

332. **Answer:** C

Explanation: 802.11g networks can handle up to 54 megabits per second, although 28 megabits per second is more typical. This is in contrast to 802.11b, which can handle up to 11 megabits per second.

333. **Answer:** B

Explanation: WEP, which stands for Wired Equivalent Privacy, was the first encryption system used to protect the confidentiality of wireless networks.

334. **Answer:** B

Explanation: WEP stands for Wired Equivalent Privacy, not Wireless Encryption Protocol, as is often mistakenly stated.

335. **Answer:** A

Explanation: The older variation of WEP encryption used a 64-bit encryption key, which is actually a 40-bit key due to export restrictions.

336. **Answer:** C

Explanation: 802.11g networks are backward compatible with 802.11b networks due to the use of the same 2.4 GHz frequency band.

337. **Answer:** B

Explanation: For 802.11b, the encoding technique is known as Complementary Code Keying (CCK), while 802.11a and 802.11g use Orthogonal Frequency-Division Multiplexing (OFDM).

338. **Answer:** C

Explanation: The IV is used to make the encryption key appear more random and is chosen by the sender to change periodically, ensuring each packet is encrypted with a different cipher stream.

339. **Answer:** B

Explanation: The WEP ICV is based on CRC-32, which is a linear function of the message. This allows an attacker to modify an encrypted message and easily adjust the ICV so the message appears authentic.

340. **Answer:** C

Explanation: The primary weakness of WEP encryption is related to IV and ICV-based attacks, which are independent of key size and allow attackers to forge packets or decrypt messages by exploiting IV reuse and weak keys.

341. **Answer:** C

Explanation: WEP, or Wired Equivalent Privacy, is used to encrypt the data transmitted over a wireless network to reduce the risk of someone passively monitoring and sniffing the wireless packets.

342. **Answer:** C

Explanation: Changing WEP keys is a manual process that becomes a monumental task for larger networks, which increases the vulnerability of the wireless LAN to eavesdroppers.

343. **Answer:** B

Explanation: 802.1x ties EAP to both wired and wireless LAN media and supports multiple authentication methods, providing a robust framework for user authentication and dynamic encryption key management.

344. **Answer:** C

Explanation: EAP with Transport Layer Security (EAP-TLS) requires mutual identity proof via public key cryptography, secured by an encrypted TLS tunnel, making it highly resistant to attacks.

345. **Answer:** B

Explanation: RADIUS serves as the authentication server in an 802.1x setup, verifying the identity of clients trying to access the network.

346. **Answer:** C

Explanation: In 802.1x terminology, the client attempting to connect is called the "supplicant."

347. **Answer:** B

Explanation: Cisco's Lightweight EAP (LEAP) requires mutual authentication, which reduces the risk of access point masquerading, a type of MitM attack.

348. **Answer:** B

Explanation: The authenticator in 802.1x terminology refers to the WAP that interfaces with the client (supplicant) and the authentication server.

349. **Answer:** B

Explanation: In typical 802.1x implementations, encryption keys can be changed automatically as frequently as necessary, which is often set to a default interval of five minutes.

350. **Answer:** C

Explanation: 802.1x provides a framework for authentication and controls user traffic but does not provide the actual authentication mechanisms; instead, it uses EAP types for that purpose.

351. **Answer:** C

Explanation: TKIP, or Temporal Key Integrity Protocol, was developed to address the vulnerabilities found in the WEP (Wired Equivalent Privacy) encryption standard. It introduced several improvements, such as key

mixing, a re-keying mechanism, and the Message Integrity Check to enhance security and correct the weak WEP problem.

352. **Answer:** B

Explanation: TKIP still uses the RC4 encryption algorithm but mitigates its weaknesses by incorporating features like key mixing, per-packet key hashing, and the Message Integrity Check (MIC), which makes it more secure than the original WEP that also used RC4.

353. **Answer:** B

Explanation: The Message Integrity Check, also known as MIC or Michael, is a part of TKIP that verifies the integrity of the data in a packet. It helps prevent an attacker from injecting data into a packet to deduce the encryption key, thus enhancing the security of the wireless network.

354. **Answer:** B

Explanation: Wi-Fi Protected Access (WPA) includes TKIP in its security protocol. WPA was an interim standard created to provide stronger security than WEP and included features like 802.1x, EAP, and TKIP. It was later succeeded by WPA2, which brought in AES as the new encryption standard.

355. **Answer:** C

Explanation: WPA-PSK, or Wi-Fi Protected Access Pre-Shared Key, refers to a mode of WPA where a shared key is used for authentication, as opposed to WPA Enterprise, which requires an external RADIUS server for authentication.

356. **Answer:** B

Explanation: WPA2 strengthens security by incorporating the AES (Advanced Encryption Standard) algorithm, providing a higher level of assurance that only authorized users can access wireless networks. It addresses the risk of WEP-based open authentication, which could be cracked by determining a single password.

357. **Answer:** A

Explanation: The IETF's 802.11i standard, which included improved security measures over its predecessors, became a full standard on July 29, 2004.

358. **Answer:** B

Explanation: A buffer overflow is a result of programming errors or techniques that fail to properly manage memory. It can be exploited by attackers to cause a denial of service, gain elevated privileges, or execute arbitrary code on a compromised system.

359. **Answer:** B

Explanation: Teleworkers and telecommuters often use Client-to-Site VPNs to remotely access the corporate network over the internet while ensuring the data is protected by encryption.

360. **Answer:** C

Explanation: Firewalls with deep packet inspection or intrusion prevention technology go beyond simple port checks and analyze the data portion of network packets to distinguish between legitimate web traffic and potential attacks, providing enhanced internet security.

361. **Answer:** B

Explanation: Penetration testing is a focused approach where the main objective is to breach the system's defenses. Unlike a vulnerability assessment, a penetration test is not about finding as many vulnerabilities as possible but rather demonstrating that an attacker can gain unauthorized access to the system or data.

362. **Answer:** C

Explanation: A vulnerability assessment is a technical probe into a system aiming to uncover all security weaknesses, including any controls that are missing or insufficient.

363. **Answer:** C

Explanation: Risk assessments are focused on understanding the potential impact on the organization, taking into account various factors, including but not limited to technical vulnerabilities.

364. **Answer:** B

Explanation: Penetration tests are technically focused and aimed at breaching defenses rather than assessing policy compliance, which is more aligned with vulnerability assessments.

365. **Answer:** C

Explanation: A vulnerability assessment is broader than a penetration test, considering not just technical vulnerabilities but also policy and procedural problems, and administrative controls.

366. **Answer:** B

Explanation: Penetration testing often involves social engineering techniques, which aim to exploit human vulnerabilities to gain unauthorized access to systems or information.

367. **Answer:** C

Explanation: A hybrid approach to security testing means integrating different methods, for example, combining risk assessment with vulnerability assessment or vulnerability assessment with penetration testing, to get a more comprehensive understanding of security posture.

368. **Answer:** C

Explanation: A vulnerability assessment is typically one of the last elements in the security life cycle, aiming to find any remaining vulnerabilities after other security measures have been implemented.

369. **Answer:** C

Explanation: A penetration test is more narrowly and technically focused than a vulnerability assessment, with the primary goal of breaking into the system to identify vulnerabilities that could be exploited.

370. **Answer:** C

Explanation: Penetration testing is described as being similar to a vulnerability assessment that did not attend to a liberal arts college buta technical school, indicating its technical and focused nature.

371. **Answer:** C

Explanation: In a pure peer-to-peer network, there is no central server managing the network, and all peers act as both clients and servers to each

other. Hybrid peer-to-peer networks have a central server that keeps information on peers.

372. **Answer:** C

Explanation: Administrative procedures related to information systems compliance include media handling, system start-up and shut-down procedures, backup requirements, system and equipment maintenance, data center access and control, contingency plans, and employee safety. Designing the graphical user interface is not mentioned as part of these responsibilities.

373. **Answer:** C

Explanation: Procedures should be developed by a technical writer who gathers relevant information from SMEs. This collaboration ensures that procedures are written efficiently and effectively, capturing the necessary expertise without burdening the SMEs, who are often busy with their day-to-day functions.

374. **Answer:** B

Explanation: The change management process is crucial for ensuring that changes to the IT infrastructure are controlled, approved, and cause minimal disruption to the processing environment and user community.

375. **Answer:** B

Explanation: Procedure writing should use an active voice to stress what has to occur and identify responsibilities clearly. A passive voice is not recommended as it can make procedures less clear.

376. **Answer:** B

Explanation: The subject matter expert should not be the one to test the procedure because they might assume information that is not present in the procedure due to their familiarity with the subject.

377. **Answer:** A

Explanation: The procurement and contracts policy should include language that requires third parties to comply with the organization's policies, procedures, and standards, including a confidentiality or nondisclosure agreement to protect sensitive information.

378. **Answer:** B

Explanation: A critical control element in the separation of duties is ensuring that the responsibility for making changes to programs or systems is separate from the responsibility of testing and updating the production environment. This helps prevent fraud and ensures quality and security.

379. **Answer:** B

Explanation: When outsourcing, the contract should include the security arrangements, service definitions, and aspects of service management to ensure that the third party delivers services that meet the organization's security standards.

380. **Answer:** A

Explanation: The contracting organization should be a member of the third-party's change management process to manage changes to the provision of the service level agreements, including maintaining and improving existing security policies, procedures, and controls.

381. **Answer:** B

Explanation: Senior Management is responsible for demonstrating support for the IS program, ensuring it has adequate resources, actively promoting the IS program, and approving policies, standards, and procedures.

382. **Answer:** D

Explanation: An effective security program includes practical security policies and procedures, quantifiable performance metrics, and consistent periodic analysis. However, eliminating all security risks is not possible; the goal is to manage and mitigate risks to an acceptable level.

383. **Answer:** B

Explanation: KPIs are designed to help an organization define and measure progress toward its goals, and they must reflect the organization's success and be quantifiable.

384. **Answer:** B

Explanation: The security administrator's role in change management is to analyze and assess the security implications of all changes before they are made to the production environment.

385. **Answer:** C

Explanation: Risk Transference involves using other options, such as purchasing insurance, to compensate for the loss associated with a risk.

386. **Answer:** B

Explanation: Vulnerability Assessments are conducted to ensure that the controls in place are effective and to evaluate the security measures, identify

deficiencies, and verify the adequacy of such measures after implementation.

387. **Answer:** B

Explanation: Time spent on an NVA is time not spent on other job functions, and costs may limit the tools available for the assessment.

388. **Answer:** C

Explanation: A technical NVA report should include a one-page summary for senior management, a general opinion section for line managers, and detailed specific vulnerability findings for technicians.

389. **Answer:** B

Explanation: Hard vulnerabilities are errors made by software companies, which can be addressed with patches such as service packs and hotfixes.

390. **Answer:** A

Explanation: The term hacker has historically referred to a computer enthusiast, and although it can have a negative connotation, it is distinct from a cracker, who is someone who attempts unauthorized access to computer systems with malicious intent.

391. **Answer:** B

Explanation: The primary role of a CISO regarding compliance and intellectual property rights is to implement specific controls and identify individual responsibilities to meet statutory, regulatory, and contractual requirements. This involves ensuring intellectual property rights like

software copyright, trademarks, patents, source code, licenses, and documentation are properly managed and compliance controls are in place.

392. **Answer:** C

Explanation: At log-on, a warning message should be presented on the computer screen indicating that the system is for authorized use only, activities will be monitored, and by completing the log-on, the user agrees to the monitoring. This helps in setting clear expectations about monitoring and authorized use.

393. **Answer:** C

Explanation: Confidentiality ensures that access to sensitive information is restricted to authorized individuals and that controls and reporting mechanisms are in place to detect problems or possible intrusions quickly and accurately. This is critical for ensuring that the information reflects the real status of the organization.

394. **Answer:** B

Explanation: Due Care refers to the care that a reasonable person would exercise under the circumstances, which is not measured by any absolute standard but depends on the relative facts of the special case.

395. **Answer:** B

Explanation: Compliance terms, such as Fiduciary Duty, Due Care, Duty of Loyalty, and more, exist to outline the legal responsibilities and rights of employees, ensuring that they act in the best interest of the organization and its stakeholders and maintain confidentiality and other ethical standards.

396. **Answer:** D

Explanation: Annual financial reports of the organization are not an element of the information security program that is presented to the audience. The key elements include reinforcing the importance of security, identifying responsible individuals, and recognizing the sensitivity and criticality of information and applications.

397. **Answer:** B

Explanation: The primary objective of an information security awareness program is to make all employees aware of their rights and responsibilities with regard to organization information assets. This includes addressing policies, procedures, and the use of tools to ensure security.

398. **Answer:** C

Explanation: Technical compliance checking involves the examination of operational systems to ensure that hardware and software controls have been correctly implemented and maintained. It covers activities such as penetration testing and vulnerability assessments.

399. **Answer:** B

Explanation: The Duty of Loyalty requires individuals to make decisions that are in the best interest of the organization, avoiding conflicts of interest and not using material inside information for personal gain.

400. **Answer:** C

Explanation: Copyright refers to a person's right to prevent others from copying works such as writings, music, and art that they have created or authored. Copyright protection is in effect for the lifetime of the author plus 95 years, ensuring long-term control over the use of their creative works.

401. **Answer:** B

Explanation: The text states that the main goal of an information security awareness program is to provide answers to the user community about what is expected of them and whom to turn to for assistance.

402. **Answer:** D

Explanation: The text suggests that there should be annual mandatory refresher classes and sessions as a part of the ongoing information security awareness program.

403. **Answer:** B

Explanation: **The**contract house should conductawareness training for its personnel rather than including them in the regular employee training sessions.

404. **Answer:** B

Explanation: The text mentions that the QWL concept introduced in the 1970s was meant to address how employees felt about their job, their bosses, and fellow employees.

405. **Answer:** C

Explanation: The "Ladder of Inference" is a concept associated with the "Learning Organization,"for the 1990s training.

406. **Answer:** C

Explanation: The suggestion is to incorporating special dates such as May 10 (International Emergency Response Day), September 8 (Computer Virus Awareness Day), and November 30 (International Computer Security Day)

should be incorporated into the calendar of events for an information security program.

407. **Answer:** B

Explanation: Effectively convey the significance of information security issues and ensure that they resonate with all who encounter the message., particularly by showing how controls help protect the employee.

408. **Answer:** B

Explanation: To assess the current level of computer usage sophistication, one suggested way is to ask questions of the audience and effectively listen to understand their needs and how they use their tools.

409. **Answer:** C

Explanation: The suggestion is to identifying potential allies by finding managers who support the security program objectives and have the respect of their peers.

410. **Answer:** B

Explanation: Before submitting a new control or policy, one should sit down with managers individually to discuss and review the change, ensuring that they are partners in the security process.

411. **Answer:** C

Explanation: The recommended maximum duration for a standard awareness presentation is 45 minutes. It should be a mix of live discussion and videotape or movie information, which is suitable for employees and line supervision.

412. **Answer:** B

Explanation: For business unit managers, who typically manage multiple departments or groups, it is recommended to schedule a 20-minute individual meeting and have two or three pages of materials to support the discussion.

413. **Answer:** A

Explanation: Senior management, including officers and directors, will generally have about 15 minutes available for the presentation. It is suggested to have a one-page summary for them.

414. **Answer:** C

Explanation: The KISS practice, which stands for Keep It Simple, Sweetie, emphasizes the importance of simplicity in delivering awareness messages and not overwhelming the audience with too much information in one session.

415. **Answer:** C

Explanation: Neural-linguistic programming identifies three basic learning styles: auditory, mechanical, and visual. Understanding these styles is crucial in communicating effectively, with visual aids being particularly important as many people are visual learners.

416. **Answer:** B

Explanation: Over 90 percent of people obtain their news and information from television or radio; thus, using a delivery model that includes videos and other visual stimuli can be effective for an awareness program.

417. **Answer:** C

Explanation: In decentralized organizations, information security coordinators are typically responsible for presenting awareness sessions to their specific unit, ensuring that the message is consistent and tailored to the unit's needs.

418. **Answer:** C

Explanation: To reinforce the security message after a presentation, providing attendees with booklets, brochures, or items with the message or slogan can be an effective reminder when they are back in their work areas.

419. **Answer:** C

Explanation: Effective communication during an awareness program involves preparing and testing all presentation materials and audio-visual equipment before the session to avoid fumbling during the presentation.

420. **Answer:** B

Explanation: The text suggests starting a session with an attention-grabbing piece, such as a simple word association personality test. This can be an effective ice-breaker to engage the audience at the beginning of the presentation.

421. **Answer:** D

Explanation: The best times for scheduling awareness sessions are in the morning on a Tuesday, Wednesday, or Thursday of a regular work week. Mondays can be hectic as people are starting their week's work, and Friday afternoons are less productive as people are winding down for the weekend.

422. **Answer:** B

Explanation: The "stunned owl" syndrome describes a situation in an awareness session where the audience is so disengaged that the words from the presenter don't seem to register with them at all.

423. **Answer:** B

Explanation: The physiological clock of humans is at its lowest productivity level right after lunch, making it a bad time to schedule an awareness session. Additionally, turning out the lights for a movie during this time might encourage snoring rather than engagement.

424. **Answer:** B

Explanation: Senior management generally prefers a short, concise presentation that quickly explains the purpose of the program, identifies problem areas, proposes solutions, and suggests an action plan. They do not typically want videos or presentation slides.

425. **Answer:** A

Explanation: When presenting to senior management, it's crucial not to go to them with a problem for which you have no solution. They are expecting you to come to them with your informed opinion on how the organization should move forward.

426. **Answer:** B

Explanation: Managers are focused on getting their jobs done and will not be interested in anything that appears to slow them down. To win them over, it is necessary to demonstrate how the new controls will improve performance processes.

427. **Answer:** B

Explanation: Line supervisors and employees tend to be skeptical about company initiatives, often hoping that they will pass without much change required of them. The compliance-checking concept will help convey that information security is a permanent and important aspect of the company.

428. **Answer:** C

Explanation: All employees have a responsibility to ensure that information assets are properly protected and are used to support management-approved activities. This is part of their role in safeguarding the organization's assets.

429. **Answer:** B

Explanation: An effective information security program should cover all information, regardless of where it is found or how it is generated. The awareness program must make this scope clear to the employees and enlist their support.

430. **Answer:** B

Explanation: For organizations with an existing outdated program, a key focus is convincing management that there is a need for change. It's also important to ensure the program benchmarks against others in the same industry or business.

431. **Answer:** C

Explanation: A disaster is defined by the Disaster Recovery Journal as "A sudden, unplanned calamitous event that brings about great damage or loss.

Any event that creates an inability on the organization's part to provide critical business functions for some undetermined period of time."

432. **Answer:** A

Explanation: An incident is defined by the DRJ as "A disruption in service that lasts less than 24 hours."

433. **Answer:** B

Explanation: Sources for understanding the latest threats can include security research organizations, vendors, and government sites.

434. **Answer:** B

Explanation: The first step is to prioritize threats based on which threats are most probable to affect the organization in terms of frequency and likelihood.

435. **Answer:** B

Explanation: A critical function of an IDS is that it can be modified to adapt to new exploits.

436. **Answer:** B

Explanation: An IDS should be able to detect any anomalies from the baseline of the organization's normal processing environment.

437. **Answer:** B

Explanation: An important aspect of an IDS system's audit logs is that they can be backed up or spooled off to another device.

438. **Answer:** C

Explanation: The role of the Information Security Manager is to manage the incident or disaster resulting from the control failure.

439. **Answer:** C

Explanation: Because the number of threats increases every year and information security budgets do not necessarily increase with the number of threats, it is necessary to prioritize which threats have the greatest potential for damage to the organization.

440. **Answer:** C

Explanation: The main goal of a BCP is to help the organization maintain operations and minimize the impact of disruptions on business functions. While IT infrastructure recovery is a part of it, the BCP encompasses the continuity of the entire business.

441. **Answer:** C

Explanation: The DRP is specifically focused on bringing up the data center and IT resources after a disaster as part of the larger Business Continuity Plan.

442. **Answer:** C

Explanation: The Information Security Steering Committee is responsible for ensuring that the BCP is tested at least on an annual basis as part of due diligence.

443. **Answer:** C

Explanation: According to NIST 800-34, the first function of executive management is to create a policy regarding BCP.

444. **Answer:** B

Explanation: The BRP specifically addresses the restoration of business processes after an emergency, not the continuity of operations during the emergency.

445. **Answer:** C

Explanation: The most common reasons for BCP failure include a lack of senior management support and high costs. Too frequent testing is not listed as a reason for failure.

446. **Answer:** B

Explanation: The COOP is focused on restoring an organization's essential functions at an alternate site for up to 30 days before returning to normal operations.

447. **Answer:** B

Explanation: The Continuity of Support Plan, which is synonymous with IT contingency planning, involves developing and maintaining plans for general support systems and major applications.

448. **Answer:** D

Explanation: The COOP is developed and executed independently from the BCP, although BCP may append it, along with BRP and DRP.

449. **Answer:** B

Explanation: A great secondary reason for BCP is that through the process, an organization will identify its critical resources, assets, and dependent systems.

450. **Answer:** C

Explanation: A Crisis Communications Plan is designed to help organizations prepare their communication strategies both internally and externally before a disaster strikes. It ensures that only approved statements are released to the public and coordinates with other plans for a consistent message.

451. **Answer: B**

Explanation: A Cyber Incident Response Plan is specifically created to enable security personnel to identify, mitigate, and recover from malicious computer incidents such as unauthorized access, denial-of-service attacks, or unauthorized changes to system hardware, software, or data.

452. **Answer:** D

Explanation: DRP stands for Disaster Recovery Plan, and it refers to a plan that is activated in the event of major, usually catastrophic, events that prevent access to the normal facility over an extended period. It typically focuses on restoring IT operations at an alternate site.

453. **Answer:** B

Explanation: The OEP provides response procedures for occupants of a facility in the event of a situation that poses a potential threat to their health and safety, the environment, or property, such as a fire, hurricane, criminal attack, or medical emergency.

454. **Answer:** C

Explanation: A Business Impact Analysis (BIA) is performed to determine which systems are most critical to an organization's operations so they can be restored in order of priority following a disruption.

455. **Answer:** C

Explanation: Performing a BIA can be difficult due to factors such as system dependencies and complexity that make it challenging to define all resources and assign criticality levels.

456. **Answer:** C

Explanation: MTO, or Maximum Tolerable Outage, is defined as the maximum duration that a system or process can be non-operational before the organization incurs significant damage or cannot recover.

457. **Answer:** C

Explanation: The results of a BIA include determining the criticality of systems and establishing Recovery Time Objectives, which are timeframes within which systems should be restored to avoid unacceptable consequences for the business.

458. **Answer:** A

Explanation: Office politics can influence the outcome of a BIA as individuals or department managers may feel that if their systems are not considered critical, their roles or departments may be viewed as expendable.

459. **Answer:** B

Explanation: One of the goals of a BIA is to quantify the impact of disruptions on business operations and to establish recovery timeframes that align with the organization's capacity to withstand downtime.

460. **Answer:** C

Explanation: A Business Impact Analysis (BIA) is performed to identify critical business processes and determine the maximum tolerable downtime for each department or process. This information is crucial for creating an effective Business Continuity Plan (BCP).

461. **Answer:** B

Explanation: Cool Sites is not a type of alternate site as per NIST 800-34. The types of alternate sites mentioned include Cold Sites, Warm Sites, Hot Sites, Mobile Sites, and Mirrored Sites.

462. **Answer:** C

Explanation: A Hot Site is an alternate site that is fully equipped to support system requirements and is typically staffed 24 hours a day, seven days a week. It is ready to receive the relocated system with minimal preparation.

463. **Answer:** C

Explanation: Reciprocal Agreements often fail because the disruptive nature of co-locating the processing on the other organization's applications makes them impractical. Despite being cost-effective, the agreements usually do not function well in practice.

464. **Answer:** D

Explanation: The Mirrored Site option provides the highest degree of availability because the data is processed and stored at the primary and alternate sites simultaneously, ensuring virtually 100 %availability.

465. **Answer:** C

Explanation: When writing a BCP, it should include information about equipment location, equipment purchase, vendor contacts, and Service Level Agreements (SLAs). These elements are crucial for the plan's implementation and success.

466. **Answer:** A

Explanation: Cross-training is important because it ensures that groups of employees can perform more than one function during a disaster. This redundancy is critical if full staff is not available due to the disaster.

467. **Answer:** B

Explanation: The initial test of a BCP plan should identify missing steps that could have been overlooked due to the in-depth knowledge of the process by the Subject Matter Expert (SME). This ensures that the plan is comprehensive and actionable.

468. **Answer:** B

Explanation: During the testing of a BCP, essential work or business processes should not be disrupted. The testing should prove the plan's effectiveness without interfering with the organization's core operations.

469. **Answer:** A

Explanation: After identifying areas for improvement in a BCP test, it is critical to assign tasks to responsible individuals, establish a timeline for completion, and review the completed tasks to ensure continuous improvement of the plan.

470. **Answer:** B

Explanation: The three phases of BCP in disaster response are the Response phase, which includes creating an emergency response plan and a crisis communications plan; the Recovery phase, where the initial portions of the business continuity plan are begun; and the Restoration phase, which is about getting processing to occur in the primary site.

471. **Answer:** B

Explanation: The Crisis Management Team is typically composed of senior executives, the public relations staff, and the human resources staff. They are assembled once an incident has happened but before it is declared a disaster.

472. **Answer:** B

Explanation: An incident only becomes a disaster after the Crisis Management Team has assessed the damage and declared it so. No recovery plans are implemented until this declaration has been made.

473. **Answer:** C

Explanation: The two key objectives during the response phase are to stabilize the environment and to protect the people involved.

474. **Answer:** A

Explanation: The offsite storage team is tasked with heading out to the storage facility to locate the tape backups of the organization's data.

475. **Answer:** C

Explanation: The salvage team goes into the disaster site to salvage any equipment that can be reused as part of the resumption level of the plan.

476. **Answer:** C

Explanation: The restoration team starts by bringing up Tier 3 to 5 applications for processing in the permanent site during the resumption phase of the plan.

477. **Answer:** A

Explanation: An incident is categorized as less severe than a disaster, often resulting in an outage that lasts 24 hours or less. A disaster implies a more significant impact and requires a formal declaration.

478. **Answer:** C

Explanation: NIST Special Publication 800-86 is one of the most commonly referenced documents for incident response, along with the "Digital Investigative Framework" by Spafford and Carrier.

479. **Answer:** C

Explanation: Upon discovering a potential security incident, the information security professional's responsibility is to report the event to senior management immediately.

480. **Answer:** B

Explanation: The primary goal of electronic surveillance is to detect changes in the system or resource usage. It can be used, for instance, to monitor if a disgruntled employee is accessing resources not needed for his normal job function or to gather evidence of computer crimes such as emailing company secrets to a competitor.

481. **Answer:** C

Explanation: eBlaster from SpectorSoft is mentioned as an example of the most popular pay surveillance utility.

482. **Answer:** B

Explanation: Insiders have typically been associated with more successful attacks compared to outsiders, as they have access to and knowledge of the system.

483. **Answer:** B

Explanation: The CIA (Central Intelligence Agency) is not listed among the law enforcement agencies mentioned for investigating computer crimes. The ones listed are the State Police, County Police, FBI, DOJ, and RCMP.

484. **Answer:** C

Explanation: Cost is repeatedly emphasized as the number one factor when it comes to running an investigation.

485. **Answer:** D

Explanation: "The Principles of Kinesic Interview and Interrogation Technique" by Stan Walters is specifically recommended for assistance with the interview and interrogation process.

486. **Answer:** B

Explanation: If all evidence points to an outsider, it is advised to look for an insider who may be assisting the outsider in making the attack successful.

487. **Answer:** D

Explanation: The principle of "Authority" involves establishing credibility quickly with claims of authority.

488. **Answer:** C

Explanation: The text mentions that 70% of reported laptop thefts can typically be recovered by an intense interrogation process of the person declaring the lost laptop.

489. **Answer:** B

Explanation: The lead investigator is like the conductor of a symphony, responsible for coordinating all the tasks during an investigation.

490. **Answer:** B

Explanation: The first cardinal rule of system seizure is "Do no harm," meaning any process used must not destroy the data on the target system.

491. **Answer:** B

Explanation: Common controls to secure the area during a system seizure include a sign-in/sign-out sheet, an evidence log, and physical controls to prevent access to the space.

492. **Answer:** B

Explanation: Capturing the contents of the monitor, even if it's just the screensaver, is important to show the state of the system when investigators approach it.

493. **Answer:** B

Explanation: There is a concern that digital images can be altered using software such as Photoshop, hence the suggestion to use film cameras or cached digital forensics cameras that create an MD5 hash of the picture.

494. **Answer:** B

Explanation: Live system forensics is often used when investigating inappropriate files, such as stolen software, company secrets, illegal images, or source code for malicious programs.

495. **Answer:** B

Explanation: According to the older forensic methodology, the CPU cache is the most volatile source of information and should be gathered first.

496. **Answer:** C

Explanation: The disadvantage of the older methodology is that it modifies the target system, which can call into question the validity of the collected evidence.

497. **Answer:** B

Explanation: Pulling the plug ensures that the operating system does not modify the contents of system files during the shutdown process, thus preserving the hard drive contents.

498. **Answer:** C

Explanation: A bit-stream image is a forensic backup that captures everything on the hard drive, including file fragments, free space, and disk space that has never been written to.

499. **Answer:** B

Explanation: After creating a bit-stream image, MD5 hash values of the original drive and the backup image are compared to ensure that the backup is an exact copy of the original without alterations.

500. **Answer:** C

Explanation: The Information Security Steering Committee typically provides strategic direction for information security within an organization. It helps ensure that information security initiatives align with business objectives and priorities.

501. **Answer:** B

Explanation: The primary objective of an information security governance framework is to align information security with business objectives. This ensures that security measures support the organization's overall goals and priorities rather than being implemented in isolation.

502. **Answer:** B

Explanation: A key component of the risk assessment process is evaluating the effectiveness of existing security controls in mitigating identified risks. This helps determine whether additional controls are needed and provides insight into the organization's overall risk posture.

503. **Answer:** B

Explanation: The purpose of a risk mitigation plan is to reduce the impact of identified risks to an acceptable level. This involves implementing measures to minimize the likelihood and severity of potential adverse events, thereby enhancing the organization's resilience to security threats.

504. **Answer:** C

Explanation: Patch management for operating systems is typically part of the technical implementation of security controls rather than the overarching information security program. It focuses on maintaining the security of IT systems by promptly applying software updates and patches to address known vulnerabilities.

505. **Answer:** C

Explanation: The primary responsibility of the Chief Information Security Officer (CISO) in managing an information security program is to ensure alignment with business goals. This involves integrating security objectives and strategies with the organization's overall mission, vision, and priorities to maximize the effectiveness of security efforts.

506. **Answer:** C

Explanation: The purpose of an incident response plan is to define the steps to take in response to security incidents. It provides a structured framework for detecting, assessing, and responding to security breaches in a timely and

effective manner, helping minimize the impact on the organization's operations and reputation.

507. **Answer:** C

Explanation: Containment is typically performed during the incident response process to prevent the spread of a security incident and limit its impact on the organization's systems and data. This involves isolating affected systems or networks to prevent further damage while the incident is investigated and resolved.

508. **Answer: A**

Explanation: Risk appetite refers to the level of risk that an organization is willing to accept or tolerate in pursuit of its objectives. It represents the maximum amount of risk that the organization considers acceptable within its risk management framework.

About Our Products

Other products from VERSAtile Reads are:

 Elevate Your Leadership: The 10 Must-Have Skills

 Elevate Your Leadership: 8 Effective Communication Skills

 Elevate Your Leadership: 10 Leadership Styles for Every Situation

 300+ PMP Practice Questions Aligned with PMBOK 7, Agile Methods, and Key Process Groups – 2024

 Exam-Cram Essentials Last-Minute Guide to Ace the PMP Exam - Your Express Guide featuring PMBOK® Guide

 Career Mastery Blueprint - Strategies for Success in Work and Business

 Memory Magic: Unraveling the Secret of Mind Mastery

 The Success Equation Psychological Foundations For Accomplishment

 Fairy Dust Chronicles – The Short and Sweet of Wonder

 B2B Breakthrough – Proven Strategies from Real-World Case Studies

CISSP Fast Track Master: CISSP Essentials for Exam Success

CISA Fast Track Master: CISA Essentials for Exam Success

www.ingramcontent.com/pod-product-compliance
Lightning Source LLC
LaVergne TN
LVHW081339050326
832903LV00024B/1209

* 9 7 9 8 3 2 6 3 2 1 2 5 1 *